Inside the mind of the bequest donor

A visual presentation of the neuroscience and psychology of effective planned giving communication

RUSSELL JAMES, J.D., PH.D.
Professor, Texas Tech University

ISBN: 1484197836
ISBN-13: 978-1484197837

CONTENTS

RUSSELL JAMES

1 PREFACE

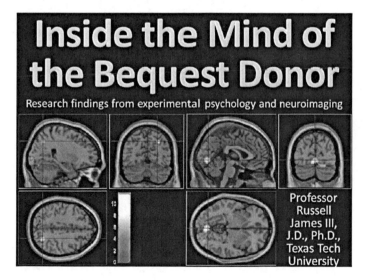

As will become readily apparent when flipping through this volume, it isn't arranged in the typical style of a book. Instead, this is an arrangement of lecture slides and related discussion that cover the concepts from research that I have been engaged in for the last several years. Why structure a book this way rather than using the traditional approach of having only text? There are a couple of reasons.

The first reason is that this type of presentation gives the reader the opportunity to engage with the material at different levels and different speeds. For example, you could certainly use this book without reading the accompanying text by simply flipping through and reading the presentation slides. Alternatively, you could flip through the slides until you reach a section of particular interest and read the related text. Of course, you could always just read it like a traditional text, including all the words. The reason I believe such flexibility is particularly important is that this book is addressed largely to those who are working in the field of planned giving. For the most part, these are busy working professionals. When time is scarce, it makes sense to provide an opportunity to simply glance through material at a rapid pace, while at the same time leaving room for more in-depth reading on each topic.

The second reason for this approach is that I have far more experience at communicating to a non-researcher audience with the use of lectures and lecture material. (Since I've been teaching college classes for 20+ years, this is not a new approach.) And although the content in this book may seem extraordinarily dry or disagreeable to you, I can assure you that my typical writing, which is intended for academic journals, is far more painful than what you will see in this book. Thus, this approach helps me to stay in a "communication" mode rather than a "technical" writing mode. It is my hope that this nontraditional format (essentially replicating the lecture format) will be helpful both to those who have a deep interest in the topic and to those who have limited time, but would like to get the gist of new research findings and frameworks.

An additional reason for this approach is my desire to include many visual elements in the presentation. Due to my work in neuroimaging research, I am able to witness the dramatic impact of presenting images, rather than pure text, on activation in the brain. If you want the brain to "wake-up", using images really helps. (Actually a thumbscrew works even better, but that's not really the kind of experience I am intending here.) Naturally, one of the central goals in presenting any kind of information is to assist the reader in not going to sleep. Perhaps the presentation of the images here will occasionally be able to break up the material in such a way that encourages continuing through the material. (Apologies also for converting the images to grayscale. Unfortunately, the cost of a full-color text on such a tiny print run as this is pretty ridiculous.)

A final reason for this format is that I am occasionally called on to deliver lectures regarding my research to a practitioner audience. Such audiences typically include fundraisers, planned giving officers, financial planners, estate planning attorneys, or others. It is inevitably the case that these opportunities for presentations are time-limited, usually about 50 minutes. And while this period of time is appropriate for the general audience, I often find that there are a few who have particular interest in the topic and for whom it would have been worthwhile to have had more time in order to allow for a more expansive discussion of topics. It is with this rare person in mind that I initially developed the concept for this project. (I hesitate to even refer to it as a book given its odd format.) For those who have attended a brief summary lecture, this represents what I might have presented if I had unlimited time and you had unlimited patience. (The requirement for unlimited patience to withstand the additional material presented here also underlies my choice of structure which makes skipping ahead fairly easy.) I hope that the structure is useful or entertaining for the reader.

As a last note of apology, those who, like me, have been subjected to legal training will note that I am not using the term "bequest" in its proper legal sense, but instead in its generic colloquial sense. After struggling for some number of years to retain the original distinctions for the terms, I have finally relented, in part because I have found that for international audiences the term "bequest" is far more recognized than any other generic descriptive terms, and that the precise legal terms provide an almost impenetrable barrier to communication. Thus, throughout this text please do not think of "bequest" in the narrow sense of personal property left by means of a will document (leading to the necessity to separately distinguish legatees, devisees, and beneficiaries), but rather as a broad term encompassing all forms of leaving a financial legacy.

This text represents an update on the ongoing process of research and learning. My life experiences have exposed me to a variety of different perspectives on the topic of charitable bequest planning. After graduating from the University of Missouri School of Law, I began working as assistant director, and then director, of planned giving at Central Christian College. Additionally, as part of my working arrangement with the college, I also maintained a private law practice, which was limited exclusively to estate planning and advising nonprofit organizations. Over the course of many years, this gave me the opportunity to see the charitable bequest planning process from the perspective of the nonprofit organization and from the perspective of the donor. Additionally, it gave me substantial experience in working with non-donors in their estate planning process.

However, during these years as a practicing estate planning attorney and director of planned giving, my academic and research interests continued to grow. I always taught an evening course each semester for the college and after many years, decided that the college professor career was my ultimate goal. In pursuit of this, I completed my PhD studies at the University of Missouri, graduating with a degree in Consumer Economics with a dissertation on the topic of charitable giving.

My research career was postponed, however, when the board of directors of Central Christian College appointed me as president of the college. As with most college presidencies, this position focused heavily on fundraising. (This was perhaps more true given that I was moving into the presidency from the development office.) Over the next 5 ½ years, we finished two major capital campaigns and started a third. We were able to build several new buildings on campus (a library and residence hall chief among them) all paid for with newly generated cash. The college was twice named as the fastest growing Christian college in the U.S. by *Christianity Today* magazine.

I relay all of this primarily to let you know that – if you work in development – I have been there. This is a volume about research findings and theoretical approaches. But, it is intensely focused of the real world of practical application. Many of the my research findings discussed here have been published in peer-reviewed academic journals. But, ultimately, my hope is to impact, not just other researchers, but the working estate planner, financial planner, fundraiser, or planned giving officer.

As I left the daily practice of fundraising and entered a faculty position at a research university (the University of Georgia), my day-to-day focus turned towards researching charitable giving and charitable bequest planning. Those years were spent mostly analyzing large secondary data sets to better understand motivations behind charitable giving and charitable bequest giving. Although that research and those findings are not the focus of this book, the knowledge gained through that process has been very helpful in identifying several important research questions explored here.

In pursuit of understanding the decision-making

processes of charitable giving and charitable bequest giving (and also in pursuit of surviving the tenure track), I published many academic journal articles. Although my research articles have appeared in academic journals in psychology, sociology, and economics, the audience of these technical journals is typically limited to other researchers. I doubt that I would be too far off in assuming that few readers of this text will have ever come across any of these (nor would I necessarily recommend doing so unless you enjoy the technical details of statistical analysis).

The next thing that happened in my career changed things substantially. I got tenure. Also, as part of an offer to get me to change universities, I received substantial research funding. So, having both tenure and initial funding I decided… to go back to school. (And you would have thought two doctorate degrees would have cured me of the "stay in school" bug!) This new training was not for the purpose of receiving additional degrees, but to learn how to develop and analyze functional magnetic resonance imaging experiments. My thought was that if we really wanted a deep understanding of how bequest decisions were made, then we would need to go beyond a "fill in the box" survey, and actually reach deep into the neurological underpinnings of the behavior.

Over the course of some years, including training at Harvard, MIT, and the MIND institute in New Mexico, I learned this new field. Also, I must give much recognition to my colleague (and co-author on some findings discussed later) Dr. Michael O'Boyle, an experienced neuroimaging researcher and founding director of the Texas Tech Neuroimaging Institute, for his years of patient explanation. As it turned out, the field of neuroimaging analysis was not so far removed from the statistical analysis I had practiced for years analyzing large longitudinal datasets. There are some differences (convolution with the hemodynamic response function, three-dimensionally related data, and a massively larger set of data), but the fundamental statistical process of detecting changes over time was quite similar. Now, after publishing several academic journal articles using functional magnetic resonance imaging (fMRI), and even teaching a graduate course in the design and analysis of fMRI experiments, I wanted to translate these results into practical terms for those who are not full-time researchers. A few months before starting this writing project I also learned of my promotion to full professor. Having run out of career ladder to climb, it seemed appropriate to peek my head out of the obscurity of academia, and share what I think we have learned so far, and how this might cause us to rethink how we encourage generosity in others.

This text presents findings from a variety of different studies, many of them mine and some of them from other researchers. All of them relate to understanding the mental, emotional and cognitive processes involved in bequest planning, in particular focusing on charitable bequest planning. This volume, however, is not a finish line, but merely a brief pause to report progress so far. We do not have final answers to many of the important questions in this area. In fact, I expect that I will never publish a "finished product" that answers all questions in this area. In this sense, I hope never to reach the status of being an "expert," but always maintain my status as a "learner" in this field. As long as there is funding and interest, I believe we will continue to learn and refine our understanding of what takes place in these decision-making processes. This text is simply a presentation of where we are at this point in time. I think it is valuable to take a moment to summarize the progress so far, because I believe that what we have learned so far, can substantially add to the tradition of simply sharing personal experiences and "war stories."

2 INTRODUCTION

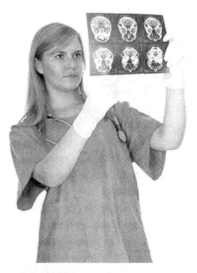

Why not just start with tips and techniques instead of going "inside the mind"?

As we begin this exploration of some of the latest research findings in this field, I think it's worthwhile to deal with one of the initial questions or objections to taking such an in-depth look at this topic. Most presentations in this field focus on a list of tips and techniques on how to accomplish different goals. There is certainly great value in learning what is being done by

8

different people at different places. However, I think it is particularly important in this field to gain a greater understanding of the underlying dynamics of how decisions are made.

Aside from the normal justifications used for a research-based methodology, I think it is particularly important in this area of charitable giving to have a research-based understanding of the processes. In other areas of fundraising or charitable giving, it is relatively easy to measure which approaches work and which approaches don't work. I can readily send out two different mailings to similar audiences and quickly measure the financial effectiveness of one mailing compared to the other. The world of current giving and fundraising provides an excellent environment in which we can conduct experiments naturally. Such experiments are relatively easy to add to the regular fundraising process.

In some ways this can make theory less relevant for other kinds of fundraising. Knowing the mechanisms of why different approaches work may not be as critical, so long as we can continue to experiment and test to ensure that what we are doing continues to work well. This is not to say that a research-based approach in fundraising in other areas is not helpful. Indeed, I've spent many years researching current giving as well and I believe that such research can be helpful. But, this is simply to point out that we can accomplish a lot in traditional "current giving" fundraising simply by experimenting and seeing the actual dollars raised as a result of those different experiments.

This happy circumstance is unfortunately not the case in the area of charitable bequest planning. In traditional charitable bequest planning, we do not have a series of gifts made year after year, but rather we have only one gift. Consequently, we cannot experiment with the same person over time and get actual dollars-in-the-door results to concretely prove which approaches are most effective. We could run an experiment on two comparable groups, just as with traditional fundraising. And, we could measure the results of those experiments. However, the "results" may take 40 years or more to come back. Consequently, the traditional trial-and-error approaches that work so well in other areas of fundraising are of relatively little value in this field. The time lags are far too long. (Certainly the time lags are far longer than the typical number of years spent at one institution by the typical planned giving officer.)

One unfortunate side effect of this environment is that ineffective approaches or ideas can become common practice for many years. Because the delay between the actions of a fundraiser attempting to encourage charitable bequests and the actual dollars received is so great, it is very difficult to change ideas that are strongly held. It also means that this segment of the industry often has an unfortunate appetite for fantasy, ranging from the way gifts are counted to absurd predictions of future transfers.

However, I believe that to the extent we can understand the mechanisms underlying why these decisions are made, and the processes by which they are made, we can dramatically improve our ability to encourage charitable bequests. And for those who care about actual long-term success in accomplishing the goals of the donor and the institution, this knowledge can become a powerful tool.

Understanding the WHY of behavior gives you the tools you need to

- Build custom approaches for your situation
- Adapt current approaches to new environments
- Understand when certain approaches won't work
- Avoid brute force trial and error (especially when each trial takes 40 years)

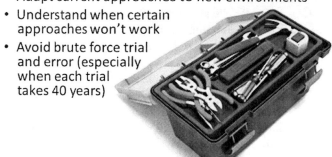

To the extent that we can improve our understanding of these processes, it gives us a set of tools far more powerful than even the best listing of tips and techniques. Even assuming that the tips and techniques we learn from others' war stories are actually effective strategies, there are often limitations to the use of these "war stories" for our own situations. Some approaches work well for one charity in one location, but would not work at all for another charity in another location. A deep understanding helps us to avoid inappropriately applying strategies from other times and other organizations, and it helps us to modify our own strategies to more effectively influence these underlying decision-making process. The reality of this field of fundraising is that brute force trial-and-error, which can work quite effectively in other areas, simply will not work in bequest giving. I just takes too long to find out what worked and what didn't work.

Someone may argue that we could measure when bequest plans are made. This is certainly true and it can be an appropriate strategy. However, we all know that a bequest plan made is not a dollar in the door. Bequest plans made can be bequest plans changed. Further, most organizations find that the bulk of all bequest dollars received come from donors who had not directly involved the charity in their estate planning processes. A substantial amount of charitable bequest dollars come from those who had not even been donors to the organization.

Consequently, we are somewhat working in the dark in this field of encouraging charitable bequest giving. Even what we are able to learn from the donors we work with directly is still knowledge about a revocable document. Ultimately, we have no concrete knowledge about a charitable bequest until the actual post-death transfer is made. Those who point to their rigorous process for documenting planned charitable bequests are conceptually in the situation of arguing that we can be more effective in nailing Jell-O to a wall if we use a heavy, 10-pound nail, than if we simply use a thumbtack. Either way, it is still nailing Jell-O to a wall. No level of documentation is going to change the reality that the documents are revocable. And thus, ultimately, we are left with the unfortunate reality that we simply do not know about the presence or amount of a charitable bequest until after the person has died. Because the ultimate results take so long before they are seen, it becomes particularly important to have a scientific basis for our marketing approaches.

Why not just ask people why they act?

They may not know

* Many processes are automatic or subconscious.

They may not tell you

* As much as 75% of survey response variation comes from wanting to appear socially acceptable (Nederhof, A., 1985.)
* This is a particular problem with giving motives

Having attempted to justify the need for a deep understanding of the processes involved in charitable bequest planning, we can now consider how we should best go about improving our understanding. Rather than using psychological theory, experiment, and neuroimaging, it is perfectly reasonable to ask, "Why don't we simply ask people why they do things?" This is, in fact, a very appropriate methodology. Later, we will use results from these type of approaches as a point of comparison with the experimental and neuroimaging results. However, simply asking people why they do what they do does not always give us a complete picture of what's really happening.

To begin with, people may simply not know the answer to the question. We don't always know why, precisely, we do the things that we do in life. Many of the processes that we use in making decisions and living our lives are automatic or subconscious. Consequently, we don't go through a rational, cognitive, step-by-step process prior to every choice.

Even when we actually engage in higher rational processing, it doesn't mean that this process ultimately drives the behavior. In neuroscience, one of the characteristics of these rational, higher cognitive, parts of the brain is that these processes are much slower than other, more deeply seated neural processes (such as emotion, fear, pain, etc.). Consequently, the higher rational parts of the brain often engage in *post hoc* rationalizations and justifications, rather than being the actual drivers of decision-making prior to the decision. This means that when we ask people for explanations of behaviors caused by automatic or subconscious processes, we are likely to get a series of after-the-fact rationalizations. Although typically plausible, these explanations may have absolutely nothing to do with the real underlying processes that actually caused the behavior.

This problem is compounded by the widespread effects of social acceptability bias. When people are asked about explanations for their past or future behavior, they are likely to provide answers with a high level of social acceptability. In other words, people tend to see themselves and their motives in the best possible light. People may be quite willing to attribute negative motivations to others, but not to themselves. Consequently, people tend to create a "halo effect" when describing their own future intentions, or their reasons for past or future behavior. In some circumstances, this bias can limit the usefulness of responses provided by individuals about why they do what they do.

This social desirability bias is especially problematic in an area such as charitable giving. Charitable giving is viewed as being a pro-social activity, and any explanations that de-emphasize this aspect will tend to be disregarded when describing personal motivations. Thus, we see repeated surveys indicating that tax benefits are not self-reported motivators for charitable giving, but simultaneously see clear evidence of the power of such benefits to dramatically alter actual giving behavior. This challenge of social acceptability bias suggests that we sometimes must go beyond simply listening to the socially acceptable answers that people might give regarding their motivations. Instead, we must consider that as one point of information to be compared against other sources of understanding. Ultimately, the goal is to actually develop a potentially deeper understanding of the underlying neural and psycho-social constructs that drive this behavior.

3 WHY BEQUEST GIVING IS DIFFERENT

Warning!
The psychological theory and neuroscience sections come first and may be a lot to get through

Promise
We will get to a range of practical applications at the end

As we begin to look at some of the underlying psychological constructs related to bequest decision-making, it is worthwhile to point out that each of these concepts will ultimately relate to concrete, practical, fundraising approaches. For those who do not have interest in psychological theory in and of itself, this area is still relevant simply because of its later practical usefulness. In later chapters, we will also spend time understanding and analyzing neuroimaging results. This was probably not the type of reading you intended to do when taking a position dealing with planned giving or estate planning. But, it turns out that understanding these processes is useful for developing practical applications in fundraising and estate planning. Hopefully based upon those assurances, you will have some level of willingness to jump into the deep end of the pool!

Bequest Giving is Different

There is a large "behavioral gap" between current giving and planned bequest giving

Let's begin with a basic statement that is fundamentally important for all of our subsequent explorations of this field. Bequest giving is different. As I have spent the last many years engaged in academic research related to current charitable giving and bequest giving it has become more and more real to me that this statement is fundamentally true. Bequest giving is a very different animal. And we will explore the details of just how different it is.

Nevertheless, we can begin with the undeniable reality that there is a massive behavioral gap between current giving activity and planned bequest giving activity. If these two types of giving were driven by the same underlying motivations, then we would see similar levels of participation. But, we do not. Current giving is an enormously widespread behavior. People give to charities and charitable causes week after week, month after month, year after year. Approximately 80% of Americans engage in this behavior each year. And yet only about 5% to 6% of the population transfers dollars to charity at death. Thus, we begin with a massive observable difference in how people behave regarding these two methodologies of transferring dollars to charity.

U.S. Over-50 Donors Giving >$500/year

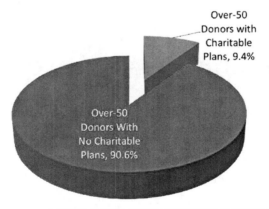

Over-50 Donors with Charitable Plans, 9.4%

Over-50 Donors With No Charitable Plans, 90.6%

* weighted nationally representative 2006 sample from Health and Retirement Study

Even among those who make regular, substantial gifts to charity, the vast majority will leave no charitable transfers at death. We can think of this from a positive perspective or a negative perspective. On the negative side the current reality means that for approximately 90% of donors, when they die their death will simply result in the termination of an income stream to the charity with no offsetting charitable bequest. Given the dramatic aging of the population, this suggests the unpleasant possibility of charitable income falling off a cliff as this massive population group ages and dies. Such a prospect cannot be attractive to any charity dependent upon their support.

Conversely, the lack of charitable bequest planning among donors also presents an enormous untapped opportunity. The bequest giving dollars we are currently seeing represent less than 10% of supporting donors. Thus, if we were able to bring bequest giving participation to the same levels seen in current giving participation, we would create a nine-fold increase in the number of donors leaving gifts at death. This means that understanding the mechanisms underlying charitable bequest donation decision-making has enormous potential benefit.

The simple lack of planning activity is a major barrier to bequest giving

As we begin to explore the differences between bequest giving and current charitable giving, a clear distinction with bequest giving is the substantial barriers to action. It is not that people conceptually have any opposition to the idea of estate planning. However, peoples' actual observed behavior suggests that there are substantial barriers. These barriers to engaging in estate planning are not necessarily external. For example, it is relatively easy to purchase a fill-in-the-blank will document from an office supply store, or even simpler to download one for little or no cost from the Internet. And although these do-it-yourself wills are not as complete or appropriate as a professionally prepared customized document, they are clearly preferable to no planning at all.

Nevertheless, despite the relative ease and simplicity of completing basic estate planning, engaging in estate planning itself is perhaps the largest barrier to charitable bequest planning. The primary cause of the lack of planning may not be external but internal. There is something about the decision mechanisms involved in the estate planning process that creates a cognitive or emotional barrier for the majority of humans.

U.S. Over 50 Population

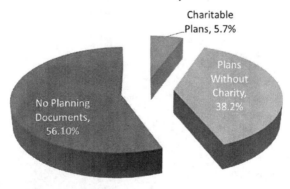

Charitable Plans, 5.7%

Plans Without Charity, 38.2%

No Planning Documents, 56.10%

* Weighted nationally representative 2006 sample

As we look at these nationally representative statistics from 2006, it gives us an understanding of just how much inaction is a barrier to bequest giving. About 6% of those over 50 have included charitable beneficiaries in their plans. About 38% of those over 50 either have not been asked or have been asked and said "no" to the question of including a charity during their planning process. But, most adults over the age of 50 do not have a charitable plan because they simply have no plan. Indeed, they cannot have a charitable plan because there are no planning documents.

The widespread reality of failing to plan does not reflect a conceptual opposition to the idea of planning as a good thing. In many surveys people will indicate a high rate of intention to eventually complete an estate plan (see, e.g., *Planned Giving in the United State 2000: A Survey of Donors* by the National Committee on Planned Giving). Very few have any objections to planning as an appropriate strategy. But it seems that this behavior is subject to infinite postponement. It is not that people believe cognitively that planning is a bad idea. Quite the opposite. People agree with the need for planning and even state intentions to, at some point, complete planning. Nevertheless, the actual estate planning behavior suggests that there is some additional barrier beyond purely rational mechanisms.

What is cognitively different about bequest decisions?

If we want to uncover the source of this extra-rational barrier behind the gap between cognitive assent to the appropriateness of estate planning and actual behavior in engaging in estate planning, we need to think about what is different about bequest decisions as compared with other legal, financial, and social decisions that we make during life. Clearly, there must be some unique characteristic of bequest decision-making that differentiates it from other kinds of decisions. There must be some distinction that causes engaging in bequest decision-making to be especially aversive or unpleasant.

- Regardless of terminology or packaging, estate planning is planning for one's own death.

- It is a strong reminder of the reality of one's own mortality.

- Experimental research has identified consistent reactions to mortality reminders.

It should not be a shock that the key distinctive characteristic of bequest decision-making that differentiates it from any number of financial, legal, and family decisions we make every day has to do with the reality of our own personal mortality. What is different about estate planning as compared with other types of financial planning is that estate planning is planning for one's own death. We can package it however we want, but ultimately estate planning asks people to engage in an extended contemplation of their own personal mortality. Very few other financial, legal, or family decisions require this type of extended mortality contemplation. Thus we might expect that this focus on personal mortality relates to the hesitancy to engage in or complete the estate planning process.

Although bequest decision-making has not been the topic of substantial academic research, it turns out to be related to a field in which much research has been completed. Specifically, there is a branch of psychology, labeled as "terror management theory," which focuses on the effects of contemplating one's own mortality. This contemplation of one's own mortality is referred to as *mortality salience*. Salience refers to the idea that something is being brought to our attention and our focus. Thus, "mortality salience" refers to an increased focus and attention being paid to the reality of one's own earthly mortality.

This line of experimental psychology research is potentially quite beneficial to those interested in understanding bequest decision-making. The intention of the researchers was not specifically related to understanding estate planning. Indeed, their purposes have more to do with understanding deep psychological constructs of the human personality. But, the experimental results produced by this line of research are often directly applicable to the bequest decision-making environment. Fundamentally, this is because the bequest decision-making environment has a high level of mortality salience. It is this mortality salience that distinguishes bequest decision-making from all other forms of financial, legal, and family-related decision making. Thus, although the original researchers purposes may have been quite different, the ultimate experimental results are directly applicable to our question of interest, which is understanding the mind of the bequest donor. Consequently, we will spend time investigating the key findings of this area of experimental psychological research.

4 TERROR MANAGEMENT THEORY
STAGE 1:
AVOIDANCE

1st Stage Defense to Mortality Reminders	2nd Stage Defense to Mortality Reminders
AVOIDANCE	**SYMBOLIC IMMORTALITY**
Avoid death reminders, e.g., deny one's vulnerability, distract oneself, avoiding self-reflective thoughts	Some part of one's self – one's family, achievements, community – will continue to exist after death (a form of autobiographical heroism)

The modern psychological field of terror management theory traces back at least as far as the writings of psychiatrist Otto Rank. Most notably in his

1932 book, *Art and Artist*, Otto Rank began to develop the concept of the importance of death contemplation in a variety of human endeavors. This stream of thought was later picked up by Ernest Becker, most pointedly in his 1973 book *The Denial of Death*. It was Becker's book that served as the genesis of the field of terror management theory. Terror management theory presents the idea that humans are the only creatures which have sufficient cognitive ability to understand that they are mortal. This comprehension or understanding of our own mortality creates an enormous difficulty for our own self or ego. This is a difficulty that other animals do not face because of their inability to contemplate and understand their own personal mortality.

The management of this understanding of our own mortality is one of the most, or perhaps the single most, important psychological tasks of humans, both individually and socially. Hence, the name of the theory, "terror management theory" refers to the management of the psychological impact of understanding our own personal mortality. For those who have a deep interest in Freudian psychology, these foundational books may be of great interest. However, for our purposes, we are most interested in the experimental results related to mortality reminders. Thus, I do not expect for the reader to become conversant with the details underlying the original theories that motivated this line of experiments. Instead, we want to examine the bottom line consequences of how mortality reminders affect people and their decisions. So whether you accept Freud, reject Freud, or could care less about Freud, is not essential for our purposes.

The essential finding of a wide range of experiments in mortality salience is that reminders of personal mortality constitute an assault on our ego, which is responded to with two stages of defenses. The first stage of defense is simple avoidance. When faced with mortality reminders, avoidance defenses involve strategies such as denying one's vulnerability, distracting oneself, avoiding self-reflective thoughts, or simply engaging in any behavior which will avoid the contemplation of one's own mortality. These first-stage defenses are rational, immediate, and relatively well perceived by the people engaging in them (at least retrospectively).

However, these first-stage defenses often do not provide complete protection against mortality salience. In some cases, external circumstances may prevent their effectiveness. Additionally, it may be that avoidance is effective only at the immediate, rational level, but not at the subconscious level. When, for whatever reason, these first-stage defenses do not protect the "self" against mortality salience, it leads to the use of second-stage defenses.

Second-stage defenses are more subconscious than first-stage avoidance. They may not even be directly perceived by the actor. Indeed, in experimental settings much of the impact of mortality salience on the use of these second-stage defenses is greater after the passage of some time following mortality reminders. The thought here is that, to the extent that second-stage defenses result from a subconscious process, the delayed impact of mortality salience on generating these second-stage defenses fits with the slower influence of the subconscious. Whereas the first-stage defense of avoidance is a relatively straightforward and immediate reaction, the second-stage defenses are a bit more involved. We will examine these second-stage defenses in more detail a bit later. For now, as a placeholder, think of these second-stage defenses as creating a form of symbolic immortality. Symbolic immortality is the idea that some part of one's self – one's family, achievements, community – will continue to exist after death. Psychologically, this can be an effective defense to the attack on the ego that results from reminders of one's own personal mortality. (Note that for those with certain religious beliefs, symbolic immortality may also refer to *actual* immortality in the sense of an afterlife.)

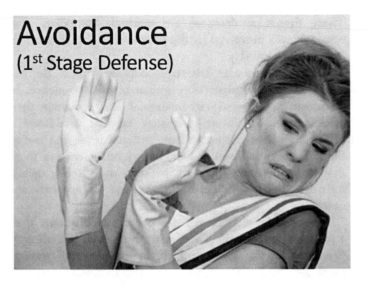

Avoidance
(1st Stage Defense)

We begin our examination of the effects of mortality reminders by looking at the first-stage defense of avoidance. This first-stage reaction is critically important for the way we develop and communicate marketing material related to charitable bequests. We will explore the practical implications of these findings later. But first we begin by examining some of the conclusions of those researchers who have spent years examining the effects of mortality reminders on human behavior.

How does the avoidance defense work? How do we see this defense play out in actual practice in human behavior? Avoidance can be seen in a wide range of behaviors, all of which have the purpose of avoiding contemplation of one's own personal mortality.

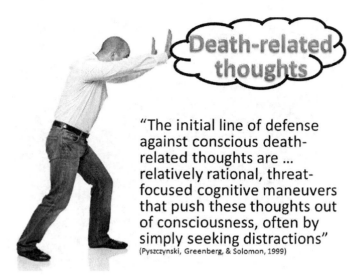

"The initial line of defense against conscious death-related thoughts are ... relatively rational, threat-focused cognitive maneuvers that push these thoughts out of consciousness, often by simply seeking distractions"
(Pyszczynski, Greenberg, & Solomon, 1999)

The fundamental goal of the initial avoidance defense is to push personal death-related thoughts out of one's mind. Simply put, thinking about one's personal mortality (i.e., mortality salience) is unpleasant and aversive. The avoidance defense attempts to reduce this unpleasant feeling by reducing mortality salience.

This first line of defense can be very much rational and intentional. The reminder of one's own mortality is a threat. We react to that threat by attempting to reduce or avoid it. As pointed out by the above quote from some of the most notable researchers in this field, one of the strategies for avoiding this type of contemplation is to simply distract oneself from the reality. Beyond this, there are a range of strategies that can be used to push these unwanted death-related thoughts out of one's mind, or at least out of one's immediate focus.

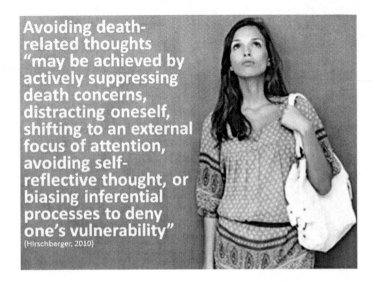

Avoiding death-related thoughts "may be achieved by actively suppressing death concerns, distracting oneself, shifting to an external focus of attention, avoiding self-reflective thought, or biasing inferential processes to deny one's vulnerability"
(Hirschberger, 2010)

This quote from Gilad Hirschberger in 2010 provides a summarization of some of the strategies used to avoid death-related thoughts. We may actively (i.e., intentionally, rationally and cognitively) suppress death concerns by focusing on why such concerns are not immediately relevant. We may engage in distraction – shifting to some other focus of attention – as a means of reducing the amount of attention being paid to the personal mortality reminder. We may simply attempt to avoid any type of self-reflective thought. Often this can be accomplished through pursuing external stimuli or external distractions. Finally, we may engage in "biasing inferential processes." In other words, we intentionally alter or misconstrue evidence so that it reduces our own sense of vulnerability in the face of mortality reminders.

Forms of Avoidance

Distract: I'm too busy to think about that right now

Differentiate: It doesn't apply to me now because I (exercise, have good cholesterol, don't smoke…)

Deny: These worries are overstated

Delay: I definitely plan to think about this… later

Depart: I am going to stay away from that reminder

We might summarize some forms of avoidance by looking at the five D's listed above. This list gives us a sense of the wide variety of strategies that we can use to avoid thinking about our own death. How do we go about doing this?

First, we can simply engage in distraction. This is the idea that, "I'm not going to deny what you're saying, but I'm too busy to think about that right now. I've got something more pressing that I have to attend to." By seeking out other, less aversive stimuli, we avoid having to engage with the source of mortality salience.

A second strategy is to differentiate ourselves from examples demonstrating our risk of mortality. For example, if someone we know dies, it creates an immediate sensation of realizing our own vulnerability. We protect against this by focusing on characteristics that differentiate the deceased person from ourselves, because if we don't differentiate between the person who has died or has had a life-threatening injury, then it exposes us to the unpleasant reality that we are also vulnerable, that we are also subject to unexpected death at any point. Those type of thoughts are naturally aversive, so we look for ways to differentiate between us and the person who experienced mortality or serious injury. If someone dies, who is otherwise similar to us or who was within our social group, we may think about how that person is different from us. For example, if someone dies of a health issue, we may think about how we exercise, but that person did not. Or, we have good cholesterol levels. Or, we don't smoke. Or, we have some characteristic that differentiates us from the person who has just died (or has experienced some serious injury posing a substantial risk of death).

Another strategy is to simply deny the concerns about mortality. Although it is difficult to completely deny our own eventual personal mortality (given the evidence of the ultimate death of all forms of life around us), we are able to protect ourselves psychologically by denying individual risks to death, especially risks of death that might come sooner rather than later. This bias will actually cause people to ignore scientific or statistical evidence about their mortality-related risks.

For example, we might see smokers engaging in the intentional denial of massive scientific evidence about the death-related effects of smoking. It is not that these smokers have any lower level of mathematical or cognitive ability, nor do they have any less ability to interpret statistical data when presented in any other frame of reference. However, when it comes to data leading to a conclusion demonstrating one's own personal mortality risk, those statistical abilities are not applied. Instead, we see a pattern of denial, concluding that mortality concerns are overstated. Of course, this tendency is not limited to smokers, but affects people in general when they contemplate their own personally-relevant mortality risks, and is often expressed in a tendency to deny such risks or to believe that the risks have been overstated.

Also related to the distraction strategy is the delay strategy. This strategy, of course, is directly applicable to the challenging realities of trying to motivate people to engage in estate planning. A common example of this defense is responding to a call to action by replying, "Yes, that's a good idea. Yes, I agree everyone should do that. But, I'm too busy right now to take care of it. I'll do that later." The underlying psychological goal here is to avoid the contemplation of one's own mortality. One way to avoid that contemplation which does not require denying one's own mortality or even denying the necessity of contemplating mortality is to simply delay the contemplation of mortality. Consequently, the enemy of estate planning, and indeed, the enemy of the charitable bequest, is not the answer of "no." Instead, the enemy is the answer of "later." We fight against this underlying psychological mechanism of delay whenever we attempt to encourage estate planning, because we are attempting to make people engage in the contemplation of their own mortality.

Whenever it is available, another strategy to avoid mortality contemplation is to simply depart from the reminder. If we can avoid mortality contemplation by simply avoiding the personal mortality reminder, this may be the easiest way to accomplish the underlying psychological goal. Obviously, the desire to depart from or avoid things which remind us of our own personal mortality will likely have a substantial impact on the effectiveness of marketing designed to get people to engage in a behavior (e.g., estate planning) that directly focuses on their own personal mortality.

"If the test says I am at risk, the test is wrong."

Those given fake test results showing they had a **serious** fictional disease rated the test as far less reliable than those told they **didn't have** the disease or that the disease was **minor**
(Landau, Greenberg, & Sullivan, 2009)

An example of this avoidance strategy was demonstrated in the research experiment from 2009 referenced above. In this experiment, the researchers found that those given fake test results showing they had a serious fictional disease rated the test as far less reliable than those told they didn't have the disease, or that the disease was minor. Participants in this study were told about a fictional disease with a made-up name and made up consequences. They were then given a "test" to see if they had this fictional disease. After getting the results showing whether or not they had this serious fictional disease, they were asked to rate the reliability of the test.

From an objective point of view, a participant's personal outcome should have made no difference in their rating of the reliability of the test. The quality of the test is the quality of the test, regardless of whether the participant happens to have been diagnosed with the disease or not. But that's not how participants rated the quality of the test. Instead, if participants were told that the test indicated that they had the disease, they rated the test as much less reliable than if they were told that the test indicated they did not have the disease. This reflects the underlying tendency to bias statistical results in such a way as to disregard our own personal risk of mortality.

Similarly, the results showed that if participants were told that they had the disease, but the disease was described as being minor (i.e., not related to any risk of mortality), the participants rated the test as more reliable. Again, we have a simple comparison between two scenarios. In both scenarios the participants were diagnosed with a disease. (In both scenarios this was a made-up disease with a made-up name.) If the disease was minor, participants believed the test to be reliable. If the disease was major (i.e., having a risk of mortality) then participants believed the test was not reliable.

These results suggest an underlying psychological tendency to think, "If the test says I am at serious risk of death, the test is wrong. If the test says I am a serious risk of a minor disease, the test is probably right." This relates to the basic tendency to avoid mortality salience. If something makes us think that we are not invincible, if it makes us think about our own mortality, then we have a tendency to engage in these statistically biasing reasoning processes which make us feel better about the results and about ourselves.

"If the driver was OK, then he drove like I would have."

"If the driver was seriously hurt, then he drove much worse than I would have."

Death reminders increased blame for victims of car accidents with serious, but not minor, injuries
(Hirschberger, 2006)

Another example of this avoidance defense against mortality salience can be seen in the results of a study published in 2006. In this study, Hirschberger found that death reminders increased the tendency to blame victims of car accidents with serious, but not minor, injuries. The experimental setup was that individuals were asked about the relative blame that should be applied to the victim of a car accident based upon a text description of the accident scenario. One group of those participating in the experiments were first asked to engage in a series of tasks that brought to mind their own personal mortality. The other group completed other tasks that were aversive, but had no relation to personal mortality. Those who had been reminded of death prior to assessing blame for the car accident victims answered the question differently than those who had not. Specifically, those who had received the death reminders were much more likely to blame the victims of serious car accidents than those who had not.

This fits with the idea that personal mortality reminders increase the desire to differentiate ourselves from those who experience death-risking traumatic injury.

In a sense, mortality reminders are an attack. This attack causes us to separate ourselves from other mortality reminders. In other words, the first-stage response to personal mortality reminders is a defensive mode where we try to push away other personal mortality reminders. In this case, the accident scenario created a reminder that we are all at risk of death or serious injury as the result of driving an automobile. By blaming the victim, participants could separate themselves from the actions of the victim and thus mentally separate themselves from the death-related risk. This attempt at separation/avoidance can be summed up in the idea that if the driver was seriously injured, then the driver was behaving differently than I would have.

Contrast this with another result from the same study. The mortality reminders did *not* change the attribution of blame to the victim if the victim was described as having only *minor* injuries. Nothing else about the accident description differed, except for the extent of the injuries of the victim. But, this difference dramatically changed the blame attributed to the victims. Why? When we are dealing with minor injuries, we are not dealing with a mortality reminder. When we are dealing with major injuries, we are dealing with a mortality reminder. Thus, it makes sense to explain this difference in attributing blame as a psychological strategy to defend against personal mortality salience. Participants were setting up a barrier between themselves and the risk of mortality when differentiating between their normal behavior and the behavior of the seriously injured victim of the car accident. No such barrier was required when considering a driver with only minor injuries. Or, to summarize, "If the driver was okay, then he drove like I would have. But, if the driver was seriously hurt, then he drove much worse than I would have."

**Example:
Organ donation**

- Life saving gift for others
- No tangible costs
- Perceived positively by society

- Strong personal death reminder

The decision to become a posthumous organ donor is one that shares many commonalities with charitable bequest decisions. The organ donation decision can be a life-saving gift that benefits other people. Like a bequest gift, it is a gift that the donor doesn't get to see the benefits of, because it is a gift that takes place after death. Further, organ donation is a gift that has no tangible costs. The donor doesn't lose anything valuable during his or her life. As a result of making this gift, it doesn't reduce the donor's income. It doesn't reduce the donor's wealth. It doesn't reduce the donor's ability to spend money on anything or to do anything for as long as the donor is alive live. (In fact, it doesn't even reduce the financial rewards to any of the donor's heirs.) Becoming an organ donor simply has no tangible economic costs.

Organ donation is also similar to charitable bequest giving, as both are perceived positively by society. Almost no one thinks that others should be discouraged from organ donation. We see it as a helpful, selfless, and pro-social action. So with all this going for it, getting people to engage in organ donation must be one of the simplest acts ever conceived!

However, there is one major negative characteristic of engaging in organ donation. Organ donation is a strong personal death reminder. In this way also, organ donation is similar to charitable bequests. Attempts to encourage organ donation may face the same challenges and barriers inherent in attempting to encourage charitable bequests. Thus, it makes sense to explore research on organ donation decisions.

What is the most common response to an organ donation request?

So how do people respond to an organ donation request? What is the typical, instinctive reaction to this question? We should consider three types of responses. First, is the response of, "Yes, I would like to donate my organs at my death." Second, is the response "No, I do not want to donate my organs at my death." And perhaps most importantly is the third option, which is neither "yes," nor "no," but is instead, "I don't want to think about it!"

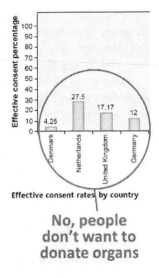

Effective consent rates by country

No, people
don't want to
donate organs

From an academic research article published in the journal *Science*, we see national results from four European countries. These results show the effective consent rate in each country to the organ donation request. If we were to describe typical preferences based upon results from these four countries, we could reasonably conclude that most people respond to the organ donation request with, "No, I do not want to donate my organs after death." However, additional evidence prevents us from claiming that this is the typical response to the question.

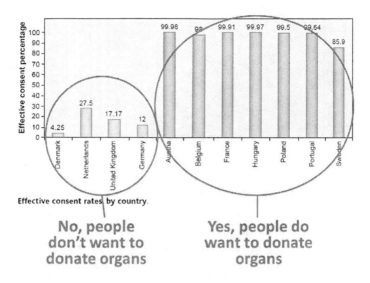

Effective consent rates by country.

No, people don't want to donate organs

Yes, people do want to donate organs

As we now look at consent rates to organ donation in a variety of other European countries we see acceptance rates near or even above 99%. If we were to look at these countries, we could reasonably conclude that the typical response to an organ donation request is, "Yes, I would like to donate my organs at death."

So how then can we resolve the conflict between these two sets of results in these two sets of countries? Before we attempt some explanation that differentiates between the countries on the left and the countries on the right based on some sociological or historical or even ethnic characteristics, let's look at what the real difference is between these two sets of countries.

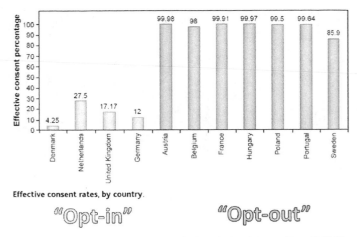

Effective consent rates, by country.

"Opt-in"   "Opt-out"

Johnson, E. J., & Goldstein, D. (2003). Do Defaults Save Lives? *Science*, 302, 1338-1339.

Here we see the important difference between the two sets of countries is not social or cultural. It is whether they have an opt-in system (the four countries on the left) or an opt-out system (the seven countries on the right). An opt-in system is one in which a person must check the box in order to opt-in to an organ donation agreement. An opt-out system is one in which a person must check the box in order to opt-out of an organ donation system. There is no meaningful difference in effort between checking the box or not checking the box. However, this simple difference in the presentation of the question produces a dramatic effect. Why might this be?

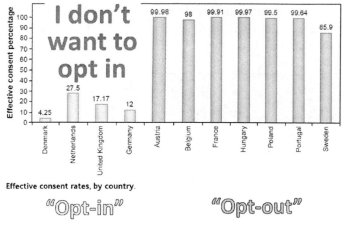

Effective consent rates, by country.

Johnson, E. J., & Goldstein, D. (2003). Do Defaults Save Lives? *Science, 302*, 1338-1339.

We can think of the results in the following way. The first set of countries provides evidence that people do not want to opt-in to an organ donation agreement.

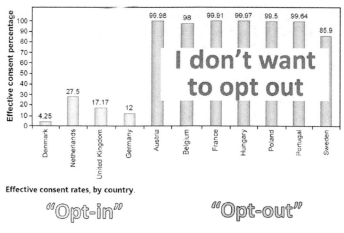

Effective consent rates, by country.

Johnson, E. J., & Goldstein, D. (2003). Do Defaults Save Lives? *Science, 302*, 1338-1339.

Results from the second set of countries provide evidence that people do not want to opt-out of an organ donation agreement. So if people do not want to opt-in to organ donation and they do not want to opt-out of organ donation, how can we reconcile these two apparently contradictory behaviors?

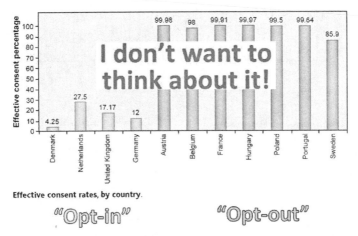

Effective consent rates, by country.

Johnson, E. J., & Goldstein, D. (2003). Do Defaults Save Lives? *Science, 302,* 1338-1339.

The two apparently contradictory behaviors can be reconciled, if the answer to the organ donation question is not "yes," or "no," but instead is "I don't want to think about it!" If the driving factor in organ donation decision-making is avoidance, then we would predict exactly the results that we see in this international comparison of behavior. Of course, this fits with the framework from experimental psychology that the first defense in the face of mortality reminders is avoidance. We want to avoid contemplation of personal mortality.

That desire for avoidance explains the apparently contradictory behavior in these results. In order to engage in an action, even an action as simple as checking a box, a person must think about, contemplate, and decide upon the issue. The easiest way to avoid that contemplation is to do nothing (perhaps justifying that we will think about it in more detail later). In this way, we delay committing to a positive action and, consequently, delay contemplating the aversive topic.

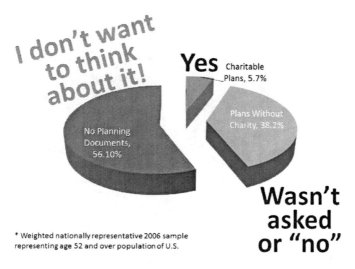

* Weighted nationally representative 2006 sample representing age 52 and over population of U.S.

In the same way that the last results displayed the dominance of the "I don't want to think about it" response in an organ donation context, we see essentially the same behavior in the charitable bequest planning context. A small portion of people respond to the question of whether or not they wish to leave a bequest to a charitable organization with the answer of "yes." Some other share of respondents either answers the question "no," or, perhaps much more commonly, are never asked the question in the first place. But, the majority responds to the question very clearly with the answer, "I don't want to think about it," as evidenced by their complete lack of planning. What we see from the experimental results related to mortality reminders, and actual behavior across many countries related to organ donations, is consistent with what we see in estate planning behavior – avoidance is the dominant response.

External realities at times break through this 1st stage avoidance defense

- Illness
- Injury
- Advancing age
- Death of a close friend
- Death of a family member
- Travel plans
- Intentionally planning for one's death through estate planning

Given the power of this first-stage defense of avoidance, we might despair that almost no one would engage in estate planning, much less charitable estate planning. However, it is critically important to understand that although avoidance is a common first-stage response to mortality reminders, it is often not a completely effective response. Avoidance is the common initial response to mortality salience and it might work in some cases, or for some period of time, but the nature of an avoidance defense is that it is not a final answer to the problem. Avoidance is simply an immediate maneuver that serves as a first-stage attempt to deal with the threat represented by mortality reminders.

But avoidance doesn't change the reality of our own undeniable personal mortality. And so, despite the best efforts at avoidance, this truth of personal mortality will often seep through into conscious and subconscious awareness.

The causes of this breaking through of mortality salience can come from a variety of sources. It might be illness, injury, advancing age, the death of a close friend or family member, travel plans, or some other external factor that breaks down the effectiveness of the avoidance barrier. At this stage avoidance no longer works to avoid contemplation of personal mortality. Attempts to distract, deny, delay, depart, or differentiate are simply no longer effective in the face of external reality.

It is at this point that second-stage defenses become much more important. These considerations are especially critical for estate planning decision-making. Once someone is at the point of engaging in estate planning for themselves, this demonstrates that he or she has broken through the first-stage "avoidance" defense. And thus, the decisions made in the estate planning process may be strongly influenced not by the first-stage issues of avoidance, but by the second-stage issues of "symbolic immortality."

Thus, in practice, both stages are important for encouraging charitable estate planning, but for different reasons. The first-stage "avoidance" is the major barrier to engaging in any form of estate planning. For that reason, it is critical to the way that we attempt to encourage estate planning. The second-stage defense is more important for the *content* of the estate plan and the *motivations* within an estate planning process. The second stage is more critical, not for whether any planning occurs, but for the potential content of those plans. We now turn to examining the second-stage defense to mortality salience.

5 TERROR MANAGEMENT THEORY STAGE TWO: AUTOBIOGRAPHICAL HEROISM & SYMBOLIC IMMORTALITY

We now consider the second-stage defense against mortality salience, which I will label using the title of "symbolic immortality."

2nd stage defense: Symbolic immortality
(a form of autobiographical heroism)

Some part of one's self - one's name, family, community, achievements, values, goals, etc. - will persist after death

The second-stage defense to mortality reminders can be thought of as an attempt to achieve symbolic immortality. The idea of symbolic immortality is that some part of one's self – one's name, family, community, achievements, values, goals, etc. – will persist after death. Mortality salience is an attack on our psychological selves. As a defense to that attack, we can focus on those parts of "ourselves" that are not mortal. To the extent that some part of "us" is not mortal, this can act as a perfect defense to the psychological crises that may result from contemplating our own finiteness. How then is this "symbolic immortality" constructed? We now turn to this question.

The "house" of autobiographical heroism requires the foundation of one's community and values which provide a framework of meaningfulness.

Symbolic immortality is in the "attic" of the "house", as it is the highest autobiographical achievement.

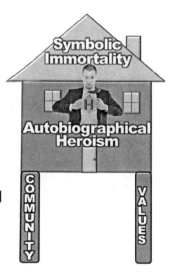

The psychological construct which we will refer to as "symbolic immortality" can best be thought of in terms of the above graphical representation. (For those who wish to go beyond this representation and interact with the more involved, sophisticated, and convoluted dimensions of the various psychological theories, I recommend to your reading Otto Rank, Ernest Becker, and the modern researchers in "terror management theory," which can be readily obtained by searching for that term in Google Scholar.) The core idea conveyed by the above image is that symbolic immortality is not a simple construct. Instead, it is better to think of it as the attic or the top of a construction. This construction, like a house, depends upon the connection with and strength of its foundations.

Symbolic immortality may be thought of as the most extreme or highest example of autobiographical heroism. Autobiographical heroism is the idea that we like to see ourselves as having positive and meaningful lives as reflected by our life stories. The greatest example of autobiographical heroism is the hero story that lives beyond the life of the hero and becomes a permanent, meaningful story within the culture of the community.

However, this idea of symbolic immortality requires a social foundation. It is not something we can construct on our own. Think, for example, of a scenario where you are on a deserted island with certain knowledge that no one would ever find you and that at the end of 20 years, you, and the island itself, would be completely destroyed and submerged into the sea as the result of a volcanic eruption. Within that framework – within that reality – it is very difficult to contemplate achieving symbolic immortality. It is difficult to imagine accomplishing something that would live beyond your own life. This is because achieving any element of symbolic immortality, at least on this earth, requires a community of others who will live on beyond your death.

It is only in the continuing existence of the community that we can achieve a measure of symbolic immortality. Although each of us will die, the community will live on. To the extent that we are able to influence our community that lives beyond us, we are then able to achieve a measure of symbolic immortality. In the same way, autobiographical heroism cannot live beyond one's death if no one else knows the story.

Thus, symbolic immortality, or any form of autobiographical heroism that will live beyond the individual's death, requires a community. And it is the values of this community that provide the underlying framework that defines meaningfulness. In the absence of meaningfulness, there can be no such thing as heroism. If we engage in what we perceive to be autobiographical heroism, but there is no community that will hear of our story, no community which shares the constructs of meaningfulness that define our life in heroic terms, then our self-perceived heroism cannot live beyond our own death. Thus, fundamentally, in order to achieve symbolic immortality, or any modicum of autobiographical heroism that will live beyond ourselves, we must rely exclusively upon the foundation of our community and community values.

It is important to understand that the term "community" here refers only to another person or group of people. It may refer to one's friends, or one's family, or one's colleagues, or those with similar interests or similar backgrounds or similar affiliations or similar ethnicity. It may ultimately refer to any group of people that one considers to be one's community. The community here consists of those considered to be an audience of importance by the person. Thus, in this context, community does not necessarily refer to one's neighborhood, municipality, or nation. (However, for many people this does define a highly relevant community.) And so it is upon the basis of this community, however we define it, that our hopes for symbolic immortality must rest.

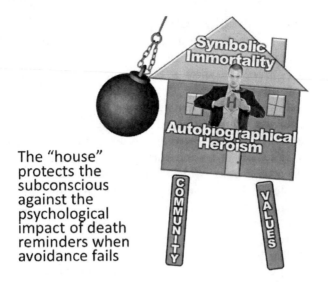

The "house" protects the subconscious against the psychological impact of death reminders when avoidance fails

Although we may be able to think about the social structures underlying our life story and meaning at any point, their relevance becomes critical when we are faced with the psychological impact of personal mortality reminders. In other words, this "house" of autobiographical heroism and symbolic immortality is like a wall of defense protecting the psychological self or ego. When we are faced with an unavoidable death reminder, that reminder acts as a wrecking ball attempting to damage our sense of psychological self. It attacks the very core of our value and meaningfulness by reminding us of our ultimate and impending finiteness. The house of symbolic immortality and autobiographical heroism can serve as a shield against this painful attack. And, so it is in the face of these death reminders that this defense becomes so critical and so important to our psychological well-being. These issues, while formerly they may have been simply in our subconscious background, become critical issues of immediate importance when we focus on our own personal mortality.

Death reminders are a psychological attack which result in greater attachment to and support of these defenses

Thus, a death reminder results in a greater attachment to and support of these defenses. When the ego is attacked, the response is to build up the defenses to protect against these attacks.

Death reminders increase desire for expressions of **symbolic immortality** and **autobiographical heroism**

Because of this defensive reaction, we expect that death reminders will increase the desire for expressions of symbolic immortality and autobiographical heroism based upon the foundation of our community and the values shared with the community. So let's now set aside, for a moment, the pure pontification of psychological theorizing and turn instead to real experimental results that demonstrate exactly how mortality salience changes the behavior, preferences, and choices of human beings.

Death reminders increase

- **Desire for fame** (Greenberg, Kosloff, Solomon, et al., 2010)
- **Interest in naming a star after one's self** (ibid)
- **Perception of one's past significance** (Landau, Greenberg, & Sullivan, 2009)
- **Likelihood of describing positive improvements when writing an autobiographical essay** (Landau, Greenberg, Sullivan, et al, 2009)
- **Perceived accuracy of a positive personality profile of one's self** (Dechesne, Pyszczynski, Janssen, et al., 2003)

Let's begin at the top half of the "house" by looking first at symbolic immortality and autobiographical heroism. How do psychology experiments measure what happens as the result of mortality salience? The typical experimental approach is to begin with two groups. One of the groups, prior to answering some outcome questions, is reminded of their personal mortality. The other group does not receive reminders of their personal mortality, but instead completes some other task unrelated to personal mortality. (Typically this control task is something that might also be considered aversive, such as, for example, answering questions about dental pain.) After this initial set of mortality reminders or some comparable non-mortality activity, both groups are then asked the same set of questions. Alternatively, responses can be compared within the same people, both before and after reminders of mortality.

These reminders of mortality can vary from experiment to experiment, but could include issues such as describing one's funeral, eliciting opinions about death, decay, and burial or reading about tragic and death-related scenarios. However, for our purposes we will put all of them under the simple heading of "death reminders." So let's review some of the results. How do death reminders change people's desires and behaviors?

To begin with, death reminders have been shown to increase people's desire for fame. As a particularly interesting example of this, death reminders have been shown to increase people's interest in having a star named after them. (In case you are interested, this is something you can get on the Internet and pay to do at websites such as www.starregistry.com. There are many, many stars, so there is no risk of running out of stars to take people's names.) These two examples: an increasing desire for fame and an increasing interest in naming a star after oneself are closely related to the idea of living beyond one's own lifetime in the memories of others. We can achieve symbolic immortality by being famous, or by having, for all eternity, a star with our own name attached to it.

Death reminders also increased people's tendency towards autobiographical heroism. For example, death reminders increased the perception of one's past significance. Death reminders also increased the likelihood of describing positive improvements throughout one's life when writing an autobiographical essay. (This is most clearly a measurement of increased autobiographical heroism in the sense that it shows an increased likelihood of writing a heroic, or at least positive, life story about one's self.) Additionally, death reminders increased the perceived accuracy of a positive personality profile of oneself. When people were given a positive assessment of their own personality profile and asked to measure the accuracy of that assessment, being reminded of one's own mortality prior to this task increased the likelihood that a person would perceive the positive personality profile as being accurate. Again, this relates to the increased desire for a positive life story or what we might call, in more colorful language, autobiographical heroism.

Death reminders are a psychological attack which result in greater attachment to and support of one's **community** and community values

As stated before, death reminders are a psychological attack on the self. This attack results in defense and support of our defensive construct referred to as symbolic immortality. For the reasons described previously, symbolic immortality, and even autobiographical heroism that will live beyond one's own life, is dependent upon the foundation of one's community and the community's values. Consequently, the defense of one's symbolic immortality "house" requires a defense and support of the foundations of the community and community values. Examples of this heightened defense of one's community and community values can be seen in a wide variety of experimental results.

Death reminders increase allegiance to one's community, such as:

- Giving among Americans to U.S. charities but not to foreign charities (Jonas, Schimel, Greenberg, et al., 2002)
- Negative ratings by Americans of anti-US essays (highly replicated)
- Negative ratings of foreign soft drinks (Friese & Hoffmann, 2008)
- Predicted number of local NFL football team wins (Dechesne, Greenberg, Arndt, et al., 2000)
- Ethnic identity among Hong Kong Chinese (Hong, Wong & Liu, 2001)
- German preference for German mark v. euro (Jonas, Fritsche, & Greenberg, 2005)

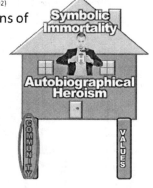

A variety of results from many different countries repeatedly support the notion that death reminders increase allegiance to one's community and community values. For example, death reminders increased giving among Americans to US charities, but they did not increase giving among Americans to foreign charities. This differential result on domestic versus foreign suggests that death reminders have a unique impact related to our own community ("in group"). In another study where American participants were asked to rate the content and quality of anti-United States essays, those who had experienced death reminders first gave much more negative ratings to the essays than those who had not. This suggests that a death reminder increases the allegiance to one's national community. At the same time, it increases resistance to those who would attack one's community. We refer to this as a defense of the "in group" and a simultaneous resistance to the "out group." Thus, death reminders make us simultaneously more pro-social and anti-social. We become much more pro-social for our "in group" while we become more antisocial for our "out group."

This "in group" allegiance can take forms that are both humorous and frightening. For example, a study in the U.S. showed that death reminders increased the predicted number of wins that the local NFL football team would have in the following season. Thus, people became more supportive of their "in group" team, and simultaneously less enamored with any "out group" teams. Similarly, death reminders increased the negative ratings of foreign soft drinks. As a somewhat humorous side effect of this "out group" resistance, people apparently decided that their taste buds were also more nationalistic following mortality reminders. These results are by no means limited to those in the United States. For example, one study showed that mortality reminders increased the ethnic identity among Hong Kong Chinese. Similarly, mortality reminders increased the German preference for the German mark currency as compared with the euro currency.

- Acceptance of negative stereotypes of residents of other cities (Renkema, et al., 2008), or nations (Schimel, et al. 1999)
- Support by Israeli participants of military action against Iran (Hirschberger, Pyszczynski & Ein-Dor, 2009)
- Support by Iranian students for martyrdom attacks against the U.S. (Pyszczynski, et al. 2006)
- Willingness of English participants to die or self-sacrifice for England (Routledge, et al, 2008)
- Dutch agreement (disagreement) with art opinions given by Dutch (Japanese) critics (Renkema, et al., 2008)
- Voting for female candidates by females, but not by males (Friese & Hoffmann, 2008)

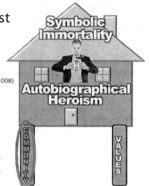

In these additional examples of the in-group/out-group effects of mortality salience, we continue to see consistent results. Mortality salience increased the acceptance of negative stereotypes of residents of other cities or other nations. This serves as another example of out-group resistance increasing along with in-group support.

Such reactions can be important in the more serious context of international conflict. For example, mortality reminders increased the support by Israelis of military action against Iran. Conversely, it increased the support by Iranian students for martyrdom attacks against the United States. In a British context, death reminders increased the willingness of English participants to die or otherwise self-sacrifice for England. Notice here as elsewhere, we are seeing examples where a support of the foundations of symbolic immortality is powerful enough to actually lead to decisions that increase or ensure the possibility of personal mortality. However, in a sense, the fear of personal mortality has been overcome by the defense of symbolic immortality.

In other, less hostile, contexts we see more examples of this same behavior. For example, following mortality salience, Dutch participants increased their agreement with art opinions given by Dutch critics while simultaneously decreasing their agreement with art opinions given by Japanese ("out group") critics. In the context of gender community, mortality salience increased voting for female candidates by females, but did not have the same effect on males.

Death reminders increased allegiance to one's "in group" (community) and resistance to "out groups"

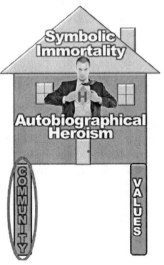

What effect might this have on bequests to charities focused on international assistance?

To summarize this group of findings, and a wide range of other findings not reported here, we can confidently say that death reminders increase allegiance to one's "in groups" and simultaneously increase resistance to one's "out-groups". Is it possible that we might be able to directly see the effects of this in a comparison of current giving and bequest giving? Can we differentiate preferred methods of giving dependent upon the charities' domestic or international focus? Although we do not have this kind of data for the United States, there is data in the United

Kingdom allowing these types of comparisons. Caritas Data, in collaboration with the Cass Business School (City University London) and professor Cathy Pharoah, publishes this data in their *Charity Market Monitor*. In the following, we examine results compiled from their 2010 *Charity Market Monitor*.

Top 100 UK fundraising charities: Average share of income from legacy gifts

26.6%

UK international relief charities (17) in top 100: Average share of income from legacy gifts

5.9%

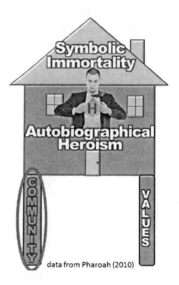

data from Pharoah (2010)

Because the data from Prof. Pharoah's research includes reports of both current and legacy gifts, we are able to compare the relative importance of these gifts for different charities. Looking just at the top 100 UK fundraising charities, i.e., those charities that raised the most total amount of money, we see a distinction among charities focused on international relief. The average share of income from legacy gifts among the top 100 UK fundraising charities was 26.6%. In contrast, the average share of income from legacy gifts among those UK international relief charities in the top 100 was only 5.9%. This does not suggest that international relief charities are not popular. Indeed 17 of the top 100 UK fundraising charities were international relief charities. People obviously support these charities with massive amounts of total donations. However, what is interesting for our purposes is that it appears there is a preference to support these charities with current dollars, but not bequest dollars. This is consistent with the idea that mortality salience increases the support for one's own community and simultaneously decreases the support for outside groups.

Although this tends to confirm the basic ideas from the psychological model, it is important not to overreact to the results. Neither the psychological model nor the results from the UK suggests that international relief charities should not care about bequest gifts. No doubt the 17 UK international relief charities referenced here would not enjoy seeing a 6% reduction in their gift income that would occur if legacy gifts stopped altogether. Further, the presence of substantial legacy gifts shows that this barrier is not an insurmountable one. But it demonstrates that this psychological model has real, bottom-line impact on charitable fundraising. Furthermore, understanding this underlying model might suggest strategies that could help, ultimately, to overcome these barriers. (One might even imagine making the beneficiaries of international charities so closely connected with donors that they too would become part of the donors "in group.")

It is certainly possible to object to the prior conclusion based on these giving results by arguing that the distinction in legacy giving relates to the cause of poverty relief in general and not specifically to the international nature of these charities. In response to this, the next set of results uses a more closely aligned comparison.

Domestic-focused children's charities in top 100 UK fundraising charities: Average share of income from legacy gifts 22.8%

Barnardo's; National Society for Prevention of Cruelty to Children; BBC Children in Need Appeal

International-focused children's charities in top 100 UK fundraising charities: Average share of income from legacy gifts 7.3%

Save the Children; Compassion UK Christian Child Development

data from Pharoah (2010)

Here we examine charities focused on supporting children and divide those charities into domestic-focused children's charities and international-focused children's charity. Here, the comparison is somewhat closer because, in both cases, we are examining charities focused upon supporting children in need. And in the context of this closer comparison, we see a similar contrast.

Among the domestic focused children's charities in the top 100 of all UK fundraising charities, the average share of income from legacy gifts was 22.8%. The international focused children's charities received only 7.3% of their gift income from legacy gifts. So we see a similar contrast here between people's preferences in current giving and legacy giving. Again, the international charities are well supported, being among the top 100 UK fundraisers. However, the preference is to support them with current giving rather than bequest giving. This is consistent with the idea that when we place people in the "mortality salience" frame of mind, they become more likely to support their in-group community and less likely to support an out-group. This is important because it takes the academic and psychological results and demonstrates their impact in real world of giving behavior. Thus, these constructs are not merely fanciful creations of research professors with too much time, but in fact describe human behavior critical to the charitable bequest decision-making process.

Death reminders are a psychological attack which result in greater attachment to and support of one's community and community values

Finally, we see additional results that support the idea that death reminders result in greater attachment to and support of one's community and also one's community values. It is not simply the community itself that a person becomes more defensive of in the face of mortality reminders, but it is also the shared values and beliefs of that community that are increasingly defended. As discussed previously, any attempt at a positive or heroic life story that will live beyond oneself depends upon the continued existence of the community and of the community values. It is the community values that provide a framework of meaningfulness that can define what is and is not positive or heroic. Although one can personally have completely independent values to define what is positive or heroic, these individual level values cannot live beyond the death of their holder unless there is a community that also accepts these values. Thus, these community values give meaning to the definition of a positive life story that could survive the death of the individual.

Death reminders increase

- Liking (disliking) for candidates of person's same (opposite) political orientation (Kosloff, Greenberg, Weise, et al., 2005)
- Punitive attitudes towards hate crimes (Lieberman, Arndt, Personius, et al., 2001)
- The amount of bond set for a prostitute (Highly replicated)
- Certainty of belief in God (Norenzayan & Hansen, 2006)

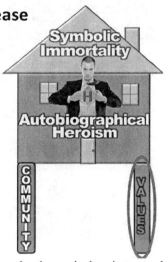

In these results, we see that death reminders increased support for one's community and community values. For example, death reminders increased participant's liking and support for candidates of their same political orientation, but also increased disliking for candidates who were not of their same political orientation.

Hate crimes are often seen as moral violations of the community's values. The amount of punishment attached to these hate crimes increased following death reminders. This again suggests the idea of increasing support and defense of community values as a result of death reminders. Similarly, in a result that has been replicated again and again in a wide range of studies, the dollar level of bond participants set as appropriate for an arrested prostitute has been shown to reliably increase following death reminders. Once again, the conclusion is that support of community values increases following death reminders. Finally, in a religious context, we see that death reminders increased the reported certainty of one's belief in God.

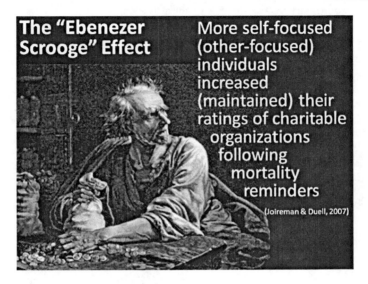

The "Ebenezer Scrooge" Effect

More self-focused (other-focused) individuals increased (maintained) their ratings of charitable organizations following mortality reminders

(Joireman & Duell, 2007)

The results of this next study are particularly instructive for those in charitable bequest planning. In 2007 Jeff Joireman and Blythe Duell, both of Washington State University, experimentally found that more self-focused individuals increased their ratings of charitable organizations following mortality reminders. Those who began the experiment being more other-focused maintained their initially higher ratings of charitable organizations in the same context. This led the authors to refer to the "Ebenezer Scrooge" effect. Following the story of Ebenezer Scrooge in *A Christmas Carol*, the self-focused miser – when faced with his own mortality – becomes charitable.

Aside from supporting the psychological basis for the Scrooge character in a Christmas Carol, this finding has important significance for practitioners in charitable bequest fund raising. It is consistent with the widespread experience of many charities that report receiving substantial bequest gifts from individuals who either supported the charity rarely and minimally, or in many cases never made a gift during life.

In stark terms, it points out the fundamental reality that charitable bequest decision-making is a different animal from current gift decision-making. Decision-making in the context of mortality salience (i.e., estate planning) will produce different results than decision-making in a normal, daily context. Thus, receiving bequest gifts from non-donors is not at all surprising, because one decision context (bequest giving) has high mortality salience and the other decision context (current giving) has no mortality salience.

This defensive reaction may help to explain significant bequests from non-donors

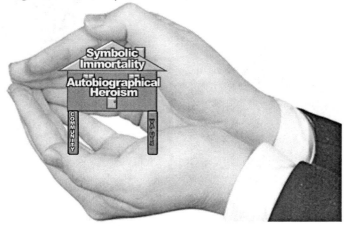

Thus, the behavior of non-donors in leaving a charitable bequest is not psychologically inconsistent. A more self-focused individual may not, as a matter of course, consider the importance of his or her community and community values. These things simply do not become a matter of focus in daily life. However, the psychological attack of a death reminder shows the clear limitations of a life completely focused on the self. The self is mortal. The self will die. If the self is all there is, then impending death is the end of all things, which is a psychologically frightening prospect. As a defense to this frightening prospect, people may engage in the construction of some form of symbolic immortality and autobiographical heroism based upon their community and its values. Thus, when faced with this threat, the importance of the community becomes immediately paramount in a way that would never happen during the distractions of daily busyness.

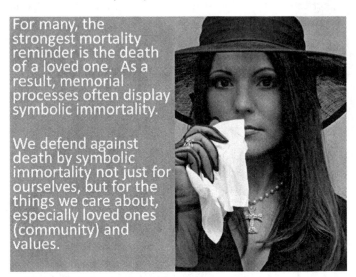

For many, the strongest mortality reminder is the death of a loved one. As a result, memorial processes often display symbolic immortality.

We defend against death by symbolic immortality not just for ourselves, but for the things we care about, especially loved ones (community) and values.

To this point we have been discussing the second-stage defense of symbolic immortality and autobiographical heroism as something that applies only to the individual himself or herself. In fact, some of the most obvious applications of this defense apply not to ourselves but to close loved ones who have died. This behavior also relates to personal mortality salience defense, even though the autobiographical heroism is applied not to oneself, but to a deceased "community" member. However, this is still important to one's own self-conception because, if other valued community members' memories can die, so can ours. By demonstrating that those important community members will continue to be remembered we can demonstrate to ourselves that we also may be remembered after our death.

This is especially critical immediately after the death of a loved one, because the death of a loved one is, by far, one of the strongest reminders of personal mortality. If we can provide some measurement of symbolic immortality for the deceased loved one, it helps to provide assurance that we, too, can achieve some level of symbolic immortality. (Or, at least that our community is capable of conveying symbolic immortality in the right circumstances.) Thus, this defensive structure of autobiographical heroism and symbolic immortality is something people will apply to deceased loved ones as well as to their own life stories. This can also be seen in a variety of common practices of memorializing the dead.

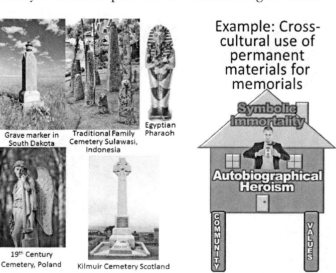

Grave marker in South Dakota

Traditional Family Cemetery Sulawasi, Indonesia

Egyptian Pharaoh

19th Century Cemetery, Poland

Kilmuir Cemetery Scotland

Example: Cross-cultural use of permanent materials for memorials

Symbolic Immortality

Autobiographical Heroism

COMMUNITY

VALUES

As visually demonstrated in the above examples, the use of permanent long-lasting materials for the construction of memorials is common across a wide range of human cultures, both modern and ancient. This is not an accidental occurrence. Rather, the use of permanent materials fits with the concept that we fight against the unfortunate reality of personal mortality by creating lasting symbols. The more important a person was to the community, the more important it is to show that they have achieved symbolic immortality. Because, if the most important people within a community are quickly forgotten, then there is no hope of achieving symbolic immortality for any members of the community, and we are again left with a world of isolation where there is no remembrance beyond our own personal mortality. Such a world is one that provides no protection against the psychological attack of the reality of personal mortality. Consequently, it is no surprise that we see cultural practices that emphasize symbolic or literal immortality across many peoples, places, and times.

Example: Speaking well of the dead by altering life stories to emphasize autobiographical heroism

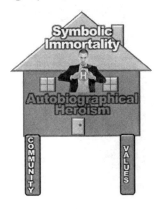

One of the most obvious and commonly experienced applications of this concept of autobiographical heroism as a defense to mortality salience can be seen in the way that the life stories of the recently and unexpectedly deceased are often immediately altered following their death. A description of the person's characteristics and life story that would have been considered completely acceptable prior to death is, by virtue of their death, immediately converted into a reality that is no longer socially acceptable. We are unwilling to convey the same kind of negative information about a person who is recently deceased. Any information or stories that contradict or interfere with the plausibility of a story of autobiographical heroism, or at a minimum a positive life impact, is deemed socially offensive.

Why is this? It may relate to the need to protect ourselves from the stark reality of personal mortality by providing a symbolic immortality defense for the recently deceased person. Perhaps we construct this protective covering of autobiographical heroism as a way of demonstrating that symbolic immortality, including some sense of autobiographical heroism, is not only possible for community members, but is normal, appropriate, and expected. This reinforces the role of the community in serving as a source of protection against complete oblivion at the point of death. For our purposes, it is yet another demonstration of the role of community-supported autobiographical heroism as a natural reaction to a mortality-salience inducing event.

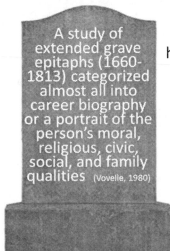

Example: Symbolically immortalizing the autobiographical heroism of the loved one

We can see a more tangible and concrete expression of this same tendency in the words used in grave epitaphs. In 1980, Michel Vovelle (University of Provence Ais-Marseille) published a study of American grave epitaphs appearing from 1660-1813. Of particular interest for our purposes is that the extended epitaphs, those going beyond simply the person's name and dates, fell into clearly delineated categories. Specifically, almost every one was either a career biography or a portrait of the person's religious, moral, civic, social, and/or family qualities. In the context of our current model, this fits cleanly with the idea of defending against mortality salience by supporting the community, the community values, and/or one's sense of autobiographical heroism. Over these centuries, when loved ones have wished to immortalize some characteristic of the deceased in an epitaph, that immortalization almost universally fell within the framework of documenting their support of the community and the community values through their life and career stories.

1st Stage Defense to Mortality Reminders	2nd Stage Defense to Mortality Reminders
AVOIDANCE	**SYMBOLIC IMMORTALITY**
Avoid death reminders, e.g., deny one's vulnerability, distract oneself, avoiding self-reflective thoughts	Some part of one's self – one's family, achievements, community – will continue to exist after death (a form of autobiographical heroism)

And so, once again, we returned to the original model. Having reviewed some samples of the evidence, both from experimental and historical studies, it appears that the model has reasonable validity for our purposes. Next, as we progress in examining results from more modern scientific analysis of neural patterns and work towards generating practical applications for charitable bequest planners, we will continue to refer back to this basic model of how humans react to mortality reminders. First, with an immediate reaction of avoidance, and when such reaction is no longer sufficient to protect against mortality reminders, then moving to a second-stage defense of pursuing symbolic immortality through a story of autobiographical heroism that supports and is supported by the community and the community's values. (In the academic literature these first-stage defenses are referred to as proximal defenses, whereas the second-stage defenses are referred to as distal defenses. However, for our discussion purposes we will try to keep the jargon to a minimum and so will continue to use the descriptions of first-stage and second-stage.)

6 UNDERSTANDING NEUROIMAGING RESEARCH IN CHARITABLE GIVING

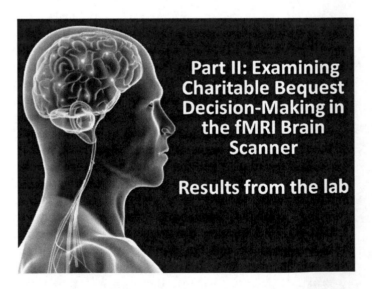

Part II: Examining Charitable Bequest Decision-Making in the fMRI Brain Scanner

Results from the lab

In this section we will shift away from the psychological and theoretical models of mortality salience and instead examine results recently generated in the lab, using functional magnetic resonance imaging (fMRI). We will examine both results that have been published from my lab and new, previously unpublished results.

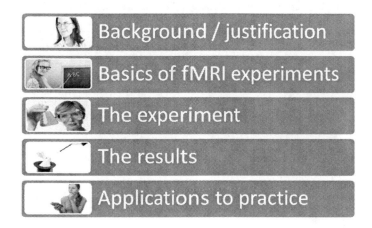

In this examination of what neuroimaging can tell us about charitable bequest decision-making, we will look at five different areas. First, we will look at justification for why the topic is worth exploring and why neuroimaging may be useful in improving our understanding of these decision making process. We will also review what has already been done in previous neuroimaging research on related topics.

Next, we will look at the basics of functional magnetic resonance imaging experiments. Although it is common practice in popular literature to skip over the realities of fMRI experiments, without this basic understanding it is easy to completely misinterpret reported results. Next, we will examine the experiments that were conducted in our lab, including all of the details about the presentations of the questions and the analysis conducted, excluding only the technical issues related to statistical analysis and image acquisition. Next, we will look at the results of these experiments. And then finally, we will shift to considering the applications of these results to the real world practice of charitable bequest fund raising.

Charitable bequests financial significance

- US charitable estate gifts over $22 billion; exceeds corporate giving of $15 billion (Giving USA, 2011).
- In prior 20 years, charitable bequests more than doubled in real dollars (Giving USA, 2011)
- Future growth from population aging and increasing propensity due to greater education and childlessness (James, Lauderdale, & Robb, 2009).

It is certainly the case that gaining a deeper understanding of bequest giving is an important goal, if only from a strictly financial perspective. Recent reports showed estate giving exceeding $22 billion annually in the United States. In comparison, this was a larger amount than all corporate giving combine.

Not only is this amount large, but it will, by all projections, continue to increase substantially over the coming years. In the last 20 years charitable bequests have more than doubled in real dollars. The next 20 to 40 years has the potential for continued dramatic increases due both to the increasing population of the older age groups, and to the increasing propensity to engage in charitable bequest planning among those in these age groups. Two of the strongest indicators for having a charitable estate plan are education levels and childlessness. Because we are able to project both the future education levels and the future childlessness rates among the age ranges that generate the bulk of all charitable estate transfers (primarily, those in their 80s and beyond), we can feel fairly confident that the propensity to leave charitable bequests will be increasing among this population, which itself will be increasing in absolute size both in the United States and in Western Europe.

Potential for greater philanthropy

- **70% to 80% of Americans engage in charitable giving each year** (Giving USA, 2011).

- **About 5% of Americans have a charitable estate plan** (James, 2009a).

Along with these already encouraging demographics, there is additional potential for even more dramatic growth in charitable bequest giving. This, of course, relates to the dramatic behavioral gap between current giving and bequest giving. To the extent that an increased understanding of bequest giving may help to close some small part of this massive gap, we could see phenomenally greater increases in charitable estate transfers in the coming years.

Challenges to encouraging bequest giving

- Unlike current giving, it is difficult to measure experimental success in bequest fundraising
- Ask to receipt may take 40+ years
- Identification of distinct cognitive characteristics could inform fundraising strategies sensitive to these differences

As discussed previously, bequest giving is an area in which traditional trial and error methodologies, which may be effective for current giving, are of limited value. Consequently, alternative methodologies for understanding the charitable bequest decision-making processes are particularly important in this area. We are, in a sense, forced to go more deeply into an understanding of the underlying neurological and psychological mechanisms, because we cannot conduct the type of quick and easy financial experiments that are possible in the field of current giving.

If, as in current giving, we could quickly experiment with different strategies and approaches, and quickly see immediate financial differences, it might be less important that we have a substantive understanding of the reasons why different strategies do and do not work. In current giving, we can see knowledge repeatedly tested, either confirming or denying our expectations, because of a continuous inflow of short-term results.

In charitable bequest giving there are almost no short-term financial results. Indeed, the time for complete results is so long as to often exceed the typical tenure of a fund-raising practitioner at a particular institution. Thus, in the area of bequest giving it is much more critical that we have accurate and scientific theoretical constructs supporting why we do what we do in fundraising practice. This need for scientifically supported theoretical constructs leads us to the current examination, attempting to explore the neurological characteristics of charitable bequest decision-making.

Previous fMRI studies in giving: reward/salience

- Moll, et al. (2006) found giving engaged mesolimbic reward systems in the same way as when subjects received monetary rewards.

- Harbaugh, Mayr, and Burghart (2007) found giving elicited neural activity in reward processing/salience areas, e.g., ventral striatum.

Although there have been no prior neuroimaging studies on the topic of charitable bequest decision-making, there have been a handful of previous studies on the topic of charitable giving. In the first neuroimaging paper on this topic Jorge Moll and colleagues found that charitable giving engaged regions referred to as mesolimbic reward systems in a way that was similar to what occurred when subjects received monetary awards. William Harbaugh and others found that giving generated neural activity in reward processing areas, specifically the ventral striatum.

It is important to note that such results are subject to

more than one interpretation. Although the regions activated are also activated as reward areas, this is not the only stimulus that causes a reaction in these areas. It is perhaps more accurate to describe these areas as being sensitive to salience (or in a non-technical sense as responding to anything that grabs our attention and focus). Thus, for example, these same areas were engaged in Harbaugh's experiment when people lost money due to forced "taxation" transfers to charities. However, we wouldn't be likely to interpret a taxation experience as a reward experience. It seems that a much more plausible account of these results is that taxation grabs our attention, and that it is this salience which is being observed in the neural activations reacting to forced taxation. Thus, there is at least a conjecture that the practice of making a charitable gift creates a reward in the mental structures in the brain, but that there are alternative interpretations for this activation.

This type of challenge is quite common in the field of neuroimaging. The brain is complex and, consequently, the same region or regions may be engaged for a variety of different reasons and for a variety of different purposes. As such, it is particularly helpful in this field to engage in what I like to call "triangulation." That is, we like to see results that fit not only with other neuroimaging results but also with results from other methodologies, including quantitative and qualitative social science research. Although neuroimaging can be quite helpful in improving our understanding of a process, it is only one piece of the puzzle.

Previous fMRI in charitable giving: social cognition

- Izuma, Saito, and Sadato (2009) found greater ventral striatum activation before a decision to donate when observers were present v. absent

- Hare, et al. (2010), found giving value calculation was driven by input from regions involved in social cognition
- Moll, et al. (2006) found decision to donate mediated by activation in areas which play key roles in social attachment and aversion

One consistent result across several neuroimaging studies of charitable giving is that charitable giving engages brain regions that are used in social cognition. In other words, neurologically, charitable giving is a social act.

This was cleverly demonstrated by Keise Izuma and colleagues in their 2009 study in which participants made a series of decisions related to making charitable gifts out of the money being paid to the participants for their involvement in the study. The screen which presented these choices also showed a video camera image of the research assistants who were observing the participants making these decisions. The research assistants were present for some of the decisions, but for some sets of the decisions, they left so that the participants saw only their empty chairs alongside the charitable giving decision choices. The researchers found that there was greater activation in the reward/salience areas, specifically the ventral striatum, when observers were present to watch the charitable decisions. This helps to confirm the social nature of charitable giving decisions. This reward difference occurred even though the observers had no relationship with either the participants or the recipient charities.

Both Todd Hare, et al. (2010) and Jorge Moll, et al. (2006), found evidence of activation in brain regions associated with social cognition, social attachment, and social aversion. However, beyond these handful of studies we know relatively little about the neurological processes involved with charitable decision-making for current gifts, and we know essentially nothing about the neurological processes involved with bequest decision-making.

Next we will take some time to review the basics of fMRI experiments. Again, such a review is important to understanding the real significance of neuroimaging results. Such results are often reported in an overly simplistic and misleading way in the popular press. To avoid this, we will take the time to walk through the core concepts necessary to intuitively understand what fMRI experiments are actually measuring.

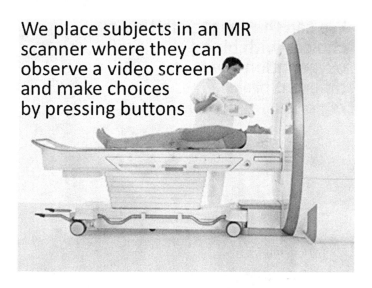

We place subjects in an MR scanner where they can observe a video screen and make choices by pressing buttons

To begin with, we placed subjects in a magnetic resonance imaging scanner. As you see in the above image, people are lying on their backs and looking straight up. The lab technician places the helmet like device seen in the above image, over the participant's head, and the moving table slides the participant's upper body into the imaging machine. Participants can see a mirror which reflects a computer screen projection. Thus, participants can view any stimuli which can be placed onto a computer screen. In addition, participants have response buttons in both hands, allowing them to make choices and selections among the different options shown on the computer screen.

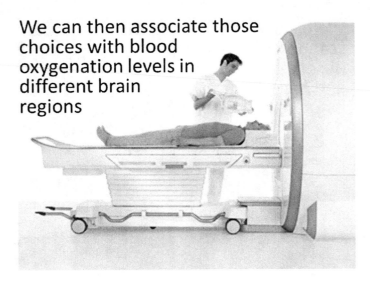

We can then associate those choices with blood oxygenation levels in different brain regions

As participants look at the various computer screens and make choices using the buttons on each hand, we can observe the differences in blood flow in different regions of the brain, thus allowing us to infer which regions of the brain are particularly engaged with the different types of decisions.

1st stage "Avoidance" is not an option, as the questions are asked directly

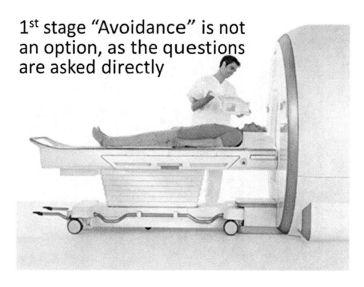

In this case, the first-stage defense of avoidance is not an available option. The bequest-related questions are asked directly to the participants and no participants refused to answer this block of questions. Consequently, we do not explore the neural correlates of avoidance, but instead explore the neural correlates of active bequest decision-making.

Subjects spend time in the scanner working with the buttons and screen to acclimate to the environment

All of this may seem to be a rather weird environment in which to make decisions or study decision-making. It is obviously not the normal, natural context in which these decisions are made. Nevertheless, as abnormal as this circumstance may initially seem, participants quickly acclimate to the environment. Before answering our questions, they have spent a substantial amount of time in the scanner, being in the environment, and even working with the buttons to familiarize themselves with the processes. (For those familiar with the processes we conduct the anatomical scan prior to any functional scans, thus allowing the participants time to acclimate to the environment.)

Now some technical details*

*Written while watching the Disney Channel with my 7 year old daughter

And now we will review some of the conceptual details of neuroimaging. However, recognizing that the readers of this text have no interest in changing their careers to pursue neuroimaging, the following is an attempt to provide a simplified story that conveys the central, critical characteristics of neuroimaging research, using a character I like to call "Vickie Voxel."

We begin with the simple idea that an fMRI picture of the brain is made up of thousands of boxes, called voxels. You may be familiar with the term pixel from a computer screen in which images are made up of individual dots called pixels. Neuro-images are also made up of these dots. However, neuro-images are three dimensional. Thus, the dots actually have volume, and are therefore called voxels, as the term "voxel" is short for "volumetric pixel."

In current neuroimaging technology these voxels are relatively small, usually about the size of one peppercorn. In our neuroimaging experiments, we used voxels that were 2x2x2 millimeters in size. Although it is possible to use smaller voxel sizes, this increases the amount of time each scan through the brain takes and consequently there are trade-offs in the quality of data obtained. At this level of resolution, we were able to take complete scans of the brain every three seconds.

Although a voxel size of 2x2x2 millimeters may seem to be a very small area of analysis, each voxel contains thousands and thousands of individual neurons. Thus, the technology is such that we are able to observe only large areas of simultaneous activation rather than individual neuron firings.

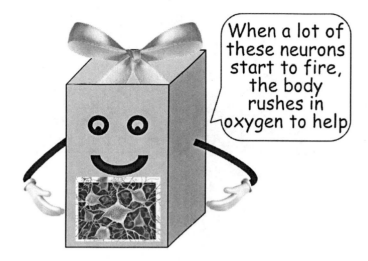

Although we cannot see individual neurons fire, we can see when a large group of neurons fires in the same area. The mechanism by which we are able to identify the firing of neurons within a voxel is by observing changes in blood oxygenation. We observe these changes because as many neurons begin to fire, the body reacts to this firing by rushing oxygen to the region to help the neurons replace the oxygen used during firing.

It is this rush of oxygen to the region that causes changes within the voxel region. Specifically, the voxel begins to change color.

The voxel becomes redder due to increased oxygenation of the blood in that region.

This increased oxygenation does not happen instantly, but takes place over several seconds as the voxel region gradually becomes more and more heavily oxygenated and consequently becomes more red.

And so, while it is not accurate to refer to areas of the

brain that "light up," it *is* accurate to refer to regions of the brain that turn more red as the result of oxygenation. It is this change in oxygenation that we observe in the fMRI machine.

The fMRI machine can see my color change because blood with a lot of oxygen (red) is less attracted to magnets than blood without much oxygen (blue).

The fMRI machine can see this color change because oxygenated blood (which is more red) is less attracted to magnets, than deoxygenated blood (which is more blue). The oxygen essentially covers the iron molecules within the blood, causing it to be less attracted to magnets. It is this difference in the para-magnetism of the tissue that an fMRI machine can observe and record.

The fMRI machine is measuring a **BOLD**
signal because the color is

Blood
Oxygen
Level
Dependent

High blood oxygen

Low blood oxygen

The signal measured by the fMRI machine is referred to as a BOLD signal, because it is Blood Oxygen Level Dependent. As blood oxygen increases, the attraction to magnetism decreases. As blood oxygen decreases, the attraction to magnetism increases.

We want to estimate the likelihood that a voxel, or group of voxels, is activated

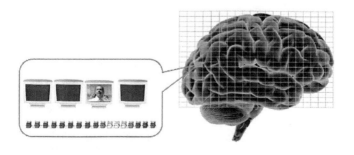

We use this BOLD signal to estimate the likelihood that a voxel or group of voxels is activated in response to some stimulus.

But, fMRI data does not start like this

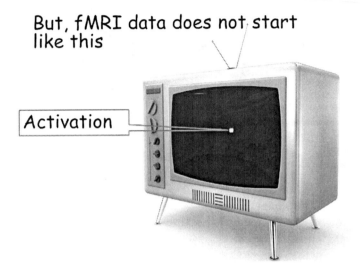

Activation

But, fMRI data does not begin in a simple form showing clear activations.

fMRI data starts like this

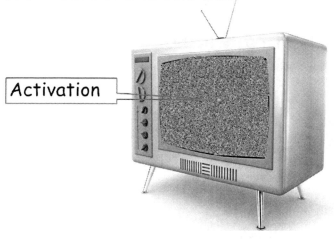

Activation

Instead, fMRI data starts out like the snow on a black-and-white television screen. It contains the signal we are interested in, but it also contains a lot of other signals that we are not interested in.

The signal is noisy

1. The brain is noisy

2. The scanner is noisy

The reasons for this noisy signal are that the brain is noisy and the scanner itself is noisy.

The brain is noisy

The brain is constantly active, constantly firing, constantly receiving input, constantly sending instructions

First, the brain is noisy. What we mean by saying that the brain is noisy is that the brain is constantly active, constantly firing, constantly receiving input, and constantly sending instructions. Although this represents real neural activations, these are not activations that we are particularly interested in. If we simply asked what regions of the brain are active when a person engages in task "X", the real answer may very well be that all regions of the brain are active. The brain is a great multi-tasker. It regulates heartbeat, blood flow, movement, vision, and body temperature. It does many, many, many things simultaneously. And the cognitive process that we may be interested in is only one of the large number of processes that the brain may be engaged in at any one point in time.

The brain is noisy

Even conscious thought is scattered. Did you think about something other than fMRI in the last 3 minutes?

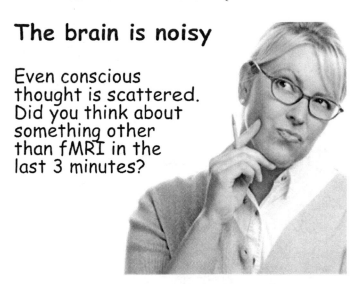

But it is not simply a matter of separating cognitive processes from other neurological processes. It is in fact the case that conscious thought itself is scattered. Even when we are trying to concentrate on something, it is a challenge to maintain that narrow focus.

So given that our brains are noisy, how do we design experiments that will give us meaningful results rather than just a pile of brain noise? We do this by employing two simultaneous strategies. The first strategy is to think in contrasts and the second is to use repetition.

Think in contrasts

Fundamentally, the most important concept to understand about neuroimaging data is that all neuroimaging results demonstrate a contrast between two or more situations. It is not fundamentally meaningful to ask, "what happens in the brain when a person is doing task X", because of the simultaneous, multi-dimensional activity of the brain. Rather, it is meaningful to ask only "what happens in the brain when a person is doing task X AS COMPARED WITH task Y".

This is a core characteristic of neuroimaging results that is often excluded from popular press reports. We deal with the constant unrelated activity in the brain by comparing what takes place during one kind of activity with what takes place during another kind of activity. By doing so, we are able to cancel out the normal activation that occurs in the brain in both conditions.

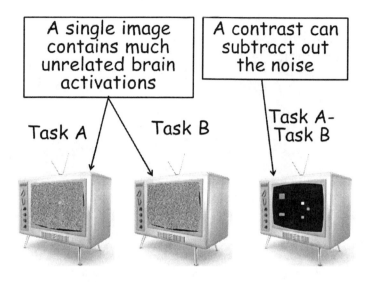

Visually, we can think about the problem in terms of an old "black-and-white" television image. If we were to look at an image of neural activation during a task, we would see the equivalent of a screen filled with white noise or "snow". When we looked at the image of a related task, we would also see an image of "snow." However, if we subtracted the second image from the first, we would, by that process, subtract out the noise and retain the activations that uniquely differentiated the first task from the second.

It is by this process that we are able to generate brain images that show activation in only a small number of regions. However, we must never forget that these brain images are not the result of neural activations during task a but are instead the result of subtracting the neural activations in one task from the neural activations in another task.

Think of study results in terms of contrasts

| Image of task A | Image of task B | Image of task A- Image of task B |

So when we read any neuroimaging results, in the popular press or otherwise, we must always think of those results in terms of contrasts comparing one activity to another.

We can use a "cognitive subtraction" comparison to isolate an activity

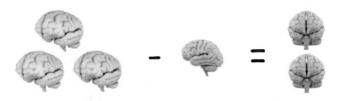

Understanding this, we then attempt to design experiments that isolate our key characteristic of interest by comparing with similar tasks that are different in small, but important, ways.

Cognitive subtraction:
the comparison task is identical, except for one variation of interest

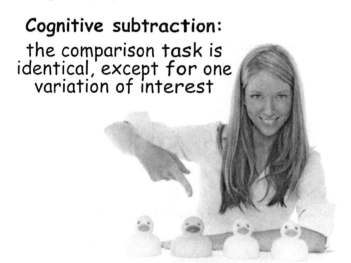

Ideally, we want to create an experimental paradigm where the comparison task is identical to the control task except for one variation of particular interest. The reason we want to create experiments like this is so that when we contrast (subtract) the images from the experimental condition and the control condition, those differences will be uniquely associated with that single variation of interest. In that way, we can more precisely understand exactly what the neuroimaging results are measuring.

The problem is that if we compare two situations which differ in many different ways, then we won't know which of these differences were related to the change in neural activation. We will only know that one of the many differences between the two conditions, or perhaps some combination of them, was responsible for the difference in neural activation. Unfortunately, this means we will have less understanding of exactly what stimulus difference generated the observed changes. Perhaps more critically is to understand that all neuroimaging data is comparison data. We do not want to make the mistake of saying, for example, "This is what happens in the brain when people engage in activity Z." Instead, we want to understand that neuroimaging experiments reveal brain activation *differences* between activity Z and activity X.

Design for repeated activations

The next critical component of neuroimaging design is that neuroimaging experiments must be designed for repeated activations. In order to be able to identify the differences between two conditions we must be able to flip back and forth between the two conditions multiple times. Ideally, we'd like to flip back and forth every 20 seconds from condition one to condition two. And, we would like to do this for an extended period of time, say, for example, eight or nine minutes. This repeated activation is important for our ultimate results. The data that we get from neuroimaging is noisy, both because there is a great deal of an uninteresting activity in the brain itself, and because of noise generated by the neuroimaging process. In order to deal with this noise. We need to have a large number of repetitions of an activity. By repeating an activity again and again and again, we can learn which parts of the image are truly related to the activity and which parts are simply unrelated noise.

This also deals with a common misunderstanding of the neuroimaging process. Some people may look at the results of a neuroimaging experiments and believe that they may just as easily be reflecting the random daydreaming that subjects engaged in while lying in the scanner. The reason why we are reasonably confident that this is not the case is because of the analysis of so many repetitions across so many participants. For example, if a participant was thinking about what he or she was going to have for lunch instead of the question on the screen in front of him or her, it is unlikely that he or she would be thinking about lunch during each of the 40 times that the experimental condition was present, and somehow, not be thinking about lunch during each of the 40 times that the comparison condition was present. In this way, the large number of repetitions helps to filter out the noise or random thoughts that are common in our cognitive processes.

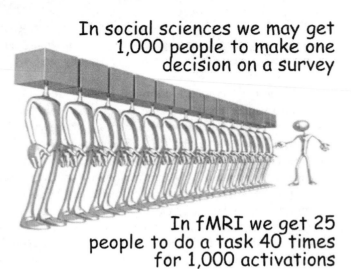

In social sciences we may get 1,000 people to make one decision on a survey

In fMRI we get 25 people to do a task 40 times for 1,000 activations

Additionally, we are able to filter out noise by comparing the activations of several different participants. Just because one participant may have been daydreaming during parts of the experiment does not pose a problem, because it is highly unlikely that the other participants were daydreaming about the same things at the same times. Thus, we are not too concerned about the effects of random noise or random thought, because the analysis focuses on those neural activations that were common across all repetitions of the particular condition and were common across all participants who were exposed to the same condition. Thus, random thoughts would only be a problem if they simultaneously occurred among most or all of the participants and additionally occurred during the experimental condition but not during the comparison condition.

This brings us to another distinction of neuroimaging research. In most social science research, we gain confidence in our results largely by increasing the number of people participating in our survey. (This is, in fact, the type of research I have been engaged in for many years, also looking at the topic of charitable bequest planning, but from a very different methodological perspective.)

However, in neuroimaging we get to a large number of observations, not by having a massive number of people scanned in the fMRI machine, but instead by having a relatively small number of people scanned who are engaging in the task of interest a large number of times. We may actually get to a similarly large number of observations in neuroimaging, but we do so with a much smaller number of participants.

Thus, it is not uncommon to see neuroimaging studies with between 12 and 35 participants. To the extent that we are interested in neural correlates that are universally shared across all humans, such a small sample is completely appropriate. However, as with all research, there is always the risk of obtaining an unusual sample that is completely distinctive from the population in general in the key characteristics of interest. Thus, as with most areas of scientific inquiry we gain confidence in results only slowly and with repeated replications produced by a variety of different researchers. Unfortunately, as the results reported here come from the first experimental inquiries into charitable bequest planning, we do not yet have a large range of replications that would increase our confidence in the results. However, to the extent that these results also correspond with findings from completely different methodologies of inquiry, we may begin to feel a bit more confident in the results as we await future replications and extensions.

7 RESULTS OF NEUROIMAGING EXPERIMENTS IN CHARITABLE BEQUEST DECISION-MAKING

The Experiment

A comparison of bequest decision making with giving and volunteering decision making

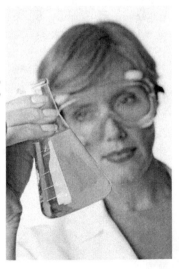

In this section we look at the experiments actually conducted in our laboratory using neuroimaging. The first set of experiments was focused on comparing bequest giving decision-making with regular giving and volunteering decision-making. As discussed previously, in neuroimaging the goal is to compare the task of interest with a control task that is similar in all ways, except for one. Thus, in this case we use the relatively similar tasks of contemplating giving and volunteering as a comparison points.

Question

What brain regions are differentially activated by bequest decisions as compared with giving and volunteering decisions?

Because there had already been previous neuroimaging experiments completed related to charitable giving, we wanted to use this as one of our comparison points. Additionally, understanding the difference between bequest giving and current giving is, ultimately, related to the central task of the inquiry. This is because there is a dramatic behavioral gap between people's propensity to engage in current giving and their propensity to engage in bequest giving. Consequently, we are particularly interested in understanding the differences between these two decision-making behaviors that might help us better understand the massive behavioral difference in the propensity to engage in the behaviors. As a final point of comparison, we also include the category of volunteering decision-making.

Exploratory expectations

- Increased activation in areas involved in death-related contemplation
- Unfortunately, very limited fMRI research on what these areas are

What did we expect find when we started this study? Because this was the first inquiry into this field of study, our expectations were consequently pretty generic. However, an obvious difference between current giving and bequest giving is that bequest giving patently involves the contemplation of one's personal death. Thus, we anticipated that there would be some neural activations distinguishing bequest giving that would relate to the death-related nature of bequest contemplation. Unfortunately, there is only very limited fMRI research on death-related contemplation.

Death-related words: precuneus

- Gündel, et al (2003) worked with subjects who had lost a first-degree relative in the previous year. The only region showing significant activation (at p<.05, FWE) in response to grief-related (v. neutral) words was the precuneus.

- Freed, et al. (2009) examined subjects who had lost a pet dog or cat within the previous 3. Four of twelve areas showing activity in response to the deceased reminder (v. neutral) words, were in the precuneus.

The line of neuroimaging research most closely related to death contemplation comes from research on the topic of grief. In particular Harald Gündel, et al., (2003), were the first to scan participants who had lost a close relative in the previous year. For purposes of that study, "close relative" referred to someone who was a first-degree relative, meaning a parent, child, or spouse. After asking subjects to describe the conditions of the deceased's final illness and funeral, the researchers then used the words from this description as "grief-related" words and contrasted the reaction to these words with the reaction to the presentation of neutral words in the scanner. Thus, the "grief-related" words, although unique to each individual, were likely to include phrases related to death, illness, and funerals. In these results, the only region showing significant activation in response to the grief-related words, as contrasted with neutral words, was a brain region known as the precuneus.

The precuneus is a brain region which we will have cause to explore in much more detail later. However, for the present, consider that this region is often engaged when a person takes an outside perspective of himself or herself. Thus, if you were to imagine yourself in a scene from the perspective of an outside observer, such an imagination might engage the precuneus region. It is possible that the grief-related words may have caused individuals to flash back to individual scenes in the hospital or funeral home where, perhaps, they envisioned the scene as an outside observer, including both themselves and the deceased in the imagined scene.

Additionally, some other research suggests that precuneus activation increases gradually as we move from envisioning a complete stranger to envisioning one who is more closely connected to us, ultimately then generating the highest activation when envisioning ourselves. This again would fit with the idea that words reminding the participants of their recently deceased loved one might bring to mind images that would activate the precuneus.

In a more recent study, Peter Freed, et al. (2009), examined those who had lost a long-time pet within the previous three months. Again, in that study, reminders of the deceased pet created activations uniquely within the precuneus region of the brain.

Methods

- Prior to entering the scanner, subjects reviewed terms along with the names and a one sentence description of each charitable organization.
- Subjects had two right and two left response buttons for each hand, for a total of four response options.
- 16 adult male subjects

For our initial study we used 16 adult male subjects. Prior to entering the scanner the participants spent time reviewing the names of all charitable organizations that would be used in the experiment along with descriptions of the purposes and activities of the organizations. In addition, participants reviewed all terms used in the study to ensure that they were familiar with the words prior to being presented with the questions. Subjects had two right hand and two left hand response buttons, giving them a total of four response options. Consequently, several of our questions involved four response options, corresponding to the four available buttons.

Comparison Questions

1. "If asked in the next 3 months, what is the likelihood you might GIVE money to _____ "
2. "If asked in the next 3 months, what is the likelihood you might VOLUNTEER time to ____ "
3. "If you signed a will in the next 3 months, what is the likelihood you might leave a BEQUEST gift to _____ "

96 questions: 3 x 28 large charitable organizations and 3 x 4 family member categories

16 second pairs (2B, 2G, 2V or 2G, 2B, 2V)

The comparison questions used in this study are listed above. There were a total of 96 questions presented to each participant. The three questions (giving, volunteering, and bequest) were asked for 28 large charitable organizations and four family member categories. Each recipient group was presented in 16-second pairs of two bequest questions or two giving questions or two volunteering questions. For each pair of organizations or individuals, the questions were presented in the sequence of two bequest questions, followed by two giving questions, followed by two volunteering questions, or, alternatively, two giving questions, followed by two bequest questions, followed by two volunteering questions. The actual recipient organizations and individuals presented in their order of presentation was as follows: UNICEF; CARE; World Wildlife Fund; The Nature Conservancy; Ducks Unlimited; National Audubon Society; Wildlife Conservation Society; a church, synagogue, mosque, and so forth; a missionary or missionary organization; a religious school (K-12); a religious college or university; a religious disaster relief organization; The YMCA; your parent or parents; your child, niece, or nephew; your brother or sister; your grandparent, aunt, or uncle; The American Cancer Society; The American Alzheimer's Association; The American Heart Association; The American Diabetes Association; Komen Breast Cancer Foundation; YWCA; Boys and Girls Clubs of America; Girl Scouts or Boy Scouts; Big Brothers/Big Sisters of America; Campus Crusade for Christ; Christian Broadcasting Network; Focus on the Family.

It may be worthwhile to discuss for a moment the reason why the questions were constructed in the way that they were. Remember, that the goal is to construct the questions so that they are as similar as possible, except for the one variation of interest. In this case, we converted all questions into a contemplation of the behavior if faced with the question in the relatively near future.

Previous studies on charitable giving using fMRI were able to examine real charitable giving decisions that involve the transfer of small amounts of funds to charitable organizations, usually taken out of the participant's payment for participating in the experiment. Thus, in that sense, the previous studies were examinations of fundamentally more "real" behavior, because the choices had actual economic consequences. However, we did not use that comparison point in this study because it is not feasible to enforce a bequest decision within an experimental environment in the same way that a current giving decision can be immediately charged. Thus, because we wanted all of the comparison points to be as similar as possible, we pushed all comparison points to contemplation of the decision in a near-term future setting.

Although it is reasonable to object that this is an analysis of contemplating future behavior rather than immediate behavior, we were most concerned with the differences between the giving, volunteering and bequest decision-making processes. Given that, what is most important is that the context between the three types is as similar as possible. In a subsequent study described later, we increased the realism and the immediacy of the decision framework for charitable estate planning using a different approach, with different points of comparison.

The Results

Behavioral Responses

Category	(1) None	(2) Unlikely	(3) Somewhat Likely	(4) Highly Likely	Missing	Avg.
Bequest	30.7%	38.9%	16.6%	11.3%	2.5%	**2.09**
Give	30.5%	28.3%	26.8%	12.7%	1.8%	**2.22**
Volunteer	24.4%	29.1%	25.8%	19.9%	0.8%	**2.42**

So what were the results of the study? First, we can look at the behavioral results. In other words, how did the participants respond to the questions presented? The above table shows the descriptive statistics for the selection of the four different response levels. It appears that the 16 second intervals allowed for the question pairs was sufficient to allow time to respond to the questions, as demonstrated by the relatively low frequency of missing responses. A missing response means that the participant did not press any of the response buttons during the period in which the question was presented on the screen. However, in the circumstance that a respondent pressed a button within one-half second of the removal of the question from the screen, this was assumed to be a response to the question, and was counted as such. It may also be that the bequest question was more challenging to contemplate given the slightly higher proportion of missing responses.

In this table, we see a similar result to the real world reality where bequest giving was less likely than current giving. Participants reported that they were less likely to leave a bequest gift as compared with their likelihood of making a current gift. Thus, the gap we see in the real world was also seen in these results. Further, these results showed a relatively good distribution among the four categories, in the sense that all categories were used in a substantial number of the responses.

It is worth noting that we were asking people to project their future behavior rather than engage in any costly behavior today. Doing so clearly increased the likelihood that responses could be subject to social acceptability bias. In other words, people tend to attribute positive or pro-social intentions or actions to themselves when responding to questions that will be observed by others. This social acceptability bias would be a great concern, if we were using these results as a method to predict the actual subsequent behavior of the participants. However, in this case we are not using the data in that way, which makes the problem less of a concern.

In other words, we are not particularly concerned

with the ability of these responses to accurately predict the actual future behavior occurring in the next three months. Instead, we are interested only with the neurological correlates for contemplating each type of behavior. And, more particularly, we are actually interested in the differences in the neural activations associated with contemplating future bequest gifts as contrasted with contemplating future current gifts or future volunteering of time. Thus, what is most critical is that the comparison is similar across all three conditions and that the comparison engages the contemplation of the three behaviors. The extent to which these responses correspond with later actual behavior is not critically relevant to the exploration here.

Core areas more engaged for bequest contemplation

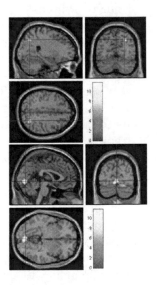

- Precuneus
- Lingual gyrus
  - Activation also increased as projected likelihood of making a charitable bequest increased

So what areas were ultimately more engaged for bequest contemplation than for charitable giving contemplation or volunteering contemplation? We will look at the specific neuroimaging results table next, but the above images show the location of the two areas of most interest specifically associated with bequest decision-making. These two areas were the precuneus and the lingual gyrus. The precuneus was mentioned before and will be covered in more detail later. The lingual gyrus is an area related to vision and visualization.

The lingual gyrus activation also increased as the projected likelihood of making a charitable bequest increased. This means that comparing the neural activations in participants when they had a high level of agreement with the bequest giving statements with their neural activations when they had a relatively low level of agreement revealed an increasing level of activation in the lingual gyrus, corresponding with the increasing level of agreement. (This is being examined in what is referred to as "parametric modulation" analysis, which was conducted separately from the comparisons of bequest and current giving.)

This type of analysis is particularly important for understanding the lingual gyrus activation. Because the lingual gyrus is a visual (and visualization) area, it is likely to respond to differences presented in the visual field. This is a concern with the initial analysis because the bequest questions were slightly longer than the comparison questions. And thus, there is some risk that the distinction between the bequest condition and the comparison conditions was generated simply by the longer length of the text.

The "parametric modulation" analysis was conducted in order to address this concern. This deals with the concern because the parametric analysis compares responses to different bequest questions. Thus, the bequest question text framework would have been identical across all bequest questions. Further, a *post hoc* analysis of the level of agreement for each recipient revealed no association between the length of the recipient name and the level of agreement. This confirms that the neural activation revealed in the "parametric modulation" analysis was not driven by different word lengths. Having eliminated this mechanism of differential activation in the lingual gyrus, the "parametric modulation" analysis still found an association between increased agreement with making a charitable bequest and increased activation in the lingual gyrus. The ultimate result of this analysis is to increase the confidence in the hypothesis that the increased lingual gyrus activation relates to the bequest giving contemplation process and not to the character length differences in the text of the questions.

As we examine the physical location of the core areas of distinction for the bequest contemplation questions, it is notable that these regions do not occur in the front of the brain. In other words, we are not seeing distinctions in the purely rational, intentional reasoning parts of the brain associated with the prefrontal cortex. Instead, we are seeing differences towards the back of the brain specifically related to visualization and self-referencing.

Activations Greater with Bequests than with Giving and/or Volunteering

(reporting only p<.05 FWE corrected cluster-level)			peak-level		cluster-level	
Contrast	Title	MNI Co-ordinates	p (FWE-corr)	Z-score	p (FWE-corr)	k_e
(1) Bequest> Give	Lingual Gyrus	-2, -78, -2	0.004	5.44	0.000	1399
	Precuneus	26, -66, 42	0.102	4.64	0.009	313
(2) Bequest> Volunteer	Lingual Gyrus	2, -80, -4	0.007	5.32	0.000	2254
	Precuneus	30, -66, 40	0.180	4.47	0.004	356
	Precentral Gyrus	-34, -3, 36	0.397	4.19	0.001	433
(3) Bequest> (Give+Volunteer)	Lingual Gyrus	0, -78, -4	0.001	5.82	0.000	2016
	Precuneus	26, -66, 42	0.007	5.33	0.001	475

Note: Using the same protocol with 37 mixed gender participants (21 female, 16 male) also peaked in lingual gyrus, precuneus, and button pushing areas

The previous chart displays the neuroimaging results for three different contrasts. First, we contrast bequest giving with current giving. Second, we contrast bequest giving with volunteering. And finally, we contrast bequest giving with both current giving and volunteering simultaneously. This displays the regions that were more active for bequest contemplation at a statistically significant level. In the first set of results, we find that only two regions were significantly more activated during bequest contemplation than during contemplation of current giving. Those two areas were the lingual gyrus and the precuneus. The lingual gyrus was activated in both the left and right hemispheres centered just slightly left of center. The precuneus activation occurred in the right hemisphere. The lingual gyrus activation was larger, activating almost 400 voxels differentially, as contrasted with the 313 voxels activated differentially in the precuneus region.

Turning to the second set of results, we see a similar outcome. Both the lingual gyrus and precuneus (in locations similar to those seen in the contrast with current giving) were more heavily activated during bequest contemplation than during volunteer contemplation. As a side note, we see that the precentral gyrus was also significantly more activated during bequest contemplation than during volunteering contemplation. However, this activation is not of interest to us, because it relates to the difference in button pushing associated with the different levels of agreement to the two questions. Consequently, we will ignore this activation for future discussions.

Finally, in the third column we compare the neural activations during bequest contemplation with those occurring during either giving or volunteering contemplation. As expected, we see similar results where both the lingual gyrus and the precuneus regions significantly increased activation during bequest contemplation. Note, that these results relate to the initial study involving 16 adult male participants. However, the same analysis was also conducted at a different time, using 21 female participants. The results of a combined analysis on all 37 participants resulted in similar outcomes, with peak activation differences in the precuneus, the lingual gyrus, and regions related to button pushing.

Areas where activation increases with greater agreement (disagreement) with the likelihood of leaving a bequest

[Linear Parametric Modulation reporting only p<.05 FWE corrected]			peak-level		cluster-level	
Contrast	Title	MNI Co-ordinates	p (FWE-corr)	Z-score	p (FWE-corr)	cluster size
(1) Increasing with agreement	**Lingual Gyrus**	10, -68, -4	0.004	5.46	0.000	671
	Postcentral Gyrus	-40, -22, 52	0.007	5.37	0.000	1200
(2) Increasing with disagreement	Precentral Gyrus	38, -20, 62	0.000	6.20	0.000	1387
	Insula	42, -20, 18	0.171	4.61	0.013	196

The previous chart showed the statistical results from the parametric modulation analysis. Here we are not contrasting bequest giving with other types of giving, but rather contrasting bequest giving contemplations where the responses were more or less positive. The first set of results shows that activation in the lingual gyrus increased with an increasing agreement to leaving a charitable bequest gift. The only other area of significantly increased activation associated with increasing agreement was a region associated with the physical act of button pushing. (Specifically, this shows greater activation in the button pushing regions of the left hemisphere which corresponds to using the right hand. The right hand was, in this study design, associated with the more positive responses. Consequently, the activations of the postcentral gyrus here and the precentral gyrus in the next analysis are both completely expected, and uninteresting.)

Although not the focus of the remainder of this text, there was also an increased activation found in the insula associated with increasing disagreement with bequest giving. This means that as resistance to making the bequest gift increased, so did activation in the insula. The insula has previously been associated with emotional responses, including negative responses such as disgust or aversion. Thus, the possibility that this activation reflects association with (negative) emotional reactions to the proposed bequest beneficiary makes sense.

The **lingual gyrus** is part of the visual system. Damage can result in losing the ability to dream (Bischof & Bassetti, 2004).

The **precuneus** has been called "the mind's eye" (Fletcher, et al., 1995), is implicated in visual imagery of memories (Fletcher, et al., 2005) and in taking a 3rd person perspective on one's self.

Visualized autobiography
visualization + 3rd person perspective on self

So what do these activations mean? Although brain regions are often associated with a range of actions, we can begin by reviewing the most common associations related to our regions of activation. The lingual gyrus is part of the visual system. Thus, it is involved in visual activity. However, the lingual gyrus has also been associated with internal visualization. For example, previous research has found that damage to the lingual gyrus can result in losing the ability to dream.

The precuneus has been called the "mind's eye" meaning that it is often engaged when we take an outsider's perspective on ourselves or our situations. If we were to look at ourselves as an outside observer, i.e., from a third-person perspective, we would potentially see increased activation in the precuneus. Corresponding with this role, the precuneus has also been implicated in the visual imagery of memories involving the self.

Combining the primary functions of the two regions suggests that what may be taking place here is a combination of visualization and a third-person perspective on one's self. In other words, it appears that the activations are consistent with a visualized autobiographical cognitive processing. Let us turn to other studies that have looked at this concept of visualized autobiography.

Visualized Autobiography

In a study where older adults were shown photographs from across their life, **precuneus** and **lingual gyrus** activation occurred when they were able to vividly relive events in the photo, but not where scenes were only vaguely familiar.

(Gilboa, et al., 2004)

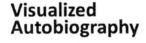

In Gilboa, et al., (2004) researchers worked with family members of older adult participants to acquire photographs taken from across the participants' lives. These photographs were not simply portrait images of the participants, but rather photographs from active scenes involving the participant. During the scanning session, participants were shown these images. The analysis compared those images which the participants rated as being vividly memorable with those images which the participants did not recall (or only vaguely recalled). In this way, the researchers were able to distinguish the special neural regions associated with vividly recalling autobiographical memories from one's own life. This vivid recollection of visual memories associated with different stages of one's life differentially activated both the precuneus and the lingual gyrus. This finding is particularly interesting for our results because it demonstrates activations in both of the regions that were differentially activated by our experiment.

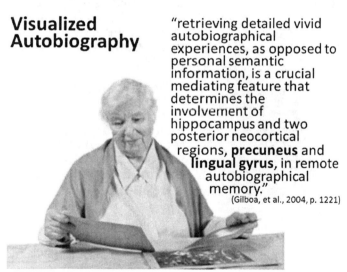

Visualized Autobiography

"retrieving detailed vivid autobiographical experiences, as opposed to personal semantic information, is a crucial mediating feature that determines the involvement of hippocampus and two posterior neocortical regions, **precuneus** and **lingual gyrus**, in remote autobiographical memory."

(Gilboa, et al., 2004, p. 1221)

In that study, the authors indicated that retrieving detailed vivid autobiographical experiences was uniquely associated with the precuneus and lingual gyrus, in addition to the hippocampus. The hippocampus is a region known to be related to memory recall. Given that the hippocampus is involved with recalling experiences, it is not necessarily a surprise that we did not see hippocampus activation associated with bequest decision-making.

Instead, it may be that what we are seeing is visualized autobiography projected into the future.

In other words, perhaps the bequest decision-making process can accurately be conceived of as the process of completing the final chapter in one's visualized autobiography. Thus, we see the activation in regions associated with vivid autobiographical experiences, but not activation in regions associated with memory recall.

Visualized Autobiography

- In Viard, et al. (2007), four of six regions showing significant activation when reliving events by mentally "traveling back in time", were in the **precuneus** and **lingual gyrus**.

- In Denkova (2006), three of the four most statistically significant regions associated with recalling autobiographical personal events were in the **lingual gyrus** and **precuneus**.

Additional evidence of this idea that bequest decision-making involves visualized autobiography projected forward into the future, comes from results associating visually traveling through time with activation in the precuneus and lingual gyrus. Specifically, in Viard, et al. (2007), four of the six regions showing significant activation when reliving events were in the precuneus and lingual gyrus. The authors referred to this as mentally "traveling back in time." Similarly, in research by Denkova, et al., (2006), three of the four most statistically significant regions associated with recalling autobiographical personal events were also in the lingual gyrus and the precuneus.

Putting all of this evidence together suggests that a simultaneous activation in the lingual gyrus and the precuneus may indicate the presence of some form of visualized autobiography. In the context of this previous research, the visualized autobiography was related to existing memories. However, in our context, we were not asking people to recall previous memories, but rather were asking them to contemplate a future action. Taking a broader perspective, we may be engaging the areas related to one's life story. The recipient of the bequest gift may relate to one's life story, which may be perceived in visual terms. Although the precise connection is not final, there does seem to be an association with these regions which previously, when combined, have been activated in tasks involving visualized autobiography.

Precuneus: Taking a 3rd person perspective on one's self

- Differentially Involved in observing one's self from an outside perspective (Vogeley & Fink, 2003)
- Greater activation when subjects described their own physical and personality traits as compared to describing another's (Kjaer, et al.,2002)
- Activation greatest when referencing one's self, lowest when referencing a neutral reference person (Lou, et al.; 2004)
- TMS disrupting normal neural circuitry in precuneus slowed ability to recall judgments about one's self more than the ability to recall judgments about others (Lou, et al., 2004)

The idea that the precuneus is particularly involved in taking a third person perspective on one's self has been demonstrated in a variety of previous research. For example, when people are asked to observe themselves from an outside perspective, this has been shown to result in activation of the precuneus. However, this activation is not limited to taking a visual outside perspective on one's self. It can also be activated when subjects are asked to describe their own physical and personality traits as compared with describing another person's traits. The description of one's own physical and personality traits differentially engages the precuneus. Another research study found that activation in the precuneus was greatest when referencing one's self, somewhat lower when referencing a person closely connected to the subject, and lowest when referencing a neutral reference person.

Finally, research using a very different methodology found even more powerful evidence for the engagement of the precuneus in self-referencing. This involved the use of transcranial magnetic stimulation (TMS). TMS uses magnetic stimulation to interfere with the normal neural activity of the brain in a small region. When interfering with normal neural activations in the precuneus region, researchers found that such interference reduced the ability to recall judgments about one's self more than the ability to recall judgments about others. This suggests that the precuneus is particularly involved with self-referential judgments, given the differential effect of precuneus interference on such cognitive processes.

Autobiography: The self across time

Inter alia, the "precuneus may respond more strongly to familiar events involving the self and possibly when the self is projected across time."
(Rabin, et al., 2009)

In Meulenbroek, et al. (2010), the precuneus was the most statistically significant region of activation for autobiographical memory tasks v. semantic true-false questions

As demonstrated in the above quotations, other researchers have previously suggested that the precuneus may be particularly involved in projecting oneself across time. Again, this is consistent with the idea that charitable bequest contemplation involves the projection of the self across time, perhaps through a mechanism appropriately described as visualizing the final chapter of one's autobiography.

It is important to note that, as this is the first inquiry into charitable bequest decision-making from a neuroimaging perspective, these hypotheses are only potential descriptions of underlying mechanisms. We have results from previous research that supports this possibility, and make it a plausible hypothesis. However, this is by no means a settled issue, rather this is simply an initial hypothesis that is consistent with previous neuroimaging results.

Lingual Gyrus: Autobiographical Visualization

"activation of the visual cortex (in the lingual gyrus) might also be related to autobiographical memory retrieval and in particular to visual imagery components, which play a key role in autobiographical memory (Greenberg & Rubin, 2003)" (D'Argembau, et al. 2007, p. 941).

The suggestion of involvement of the lingual gyrus in autobiographical visualization is also not a new one. As seen above, researchers have previously suggested that activation in this region plausibly relates to visual imagery of one's autobiographical memory.

Visual autobiography in practice

In her 2011 dissertation, Routley identified the importance of autobiographical connection when interviewing donors with planned bequests, writing, **"Indeed, when discussing which charities they had chosen to remember, there was a clear link with the life narratives of many respondents"**

Ideally, a proposed hypothesis that is consistent with neuroimaging results should also be confirmed by other findings using other methodologies. So what then might this hypothesis of visual autobiography look like in practice? Claire Routley in her 2011 doctoral dissertation completed a qualitative study resulting from interviewing a number of older adults who had made charitable bequest plans. In summarizing the findings of her qualitative, in-depth interviews, Routley specifically emphasized the links between the charities selected and the autobiographical stories of the respondents. We will explore in more detail some representative statements from this research. However, this summary result suggests a potential connection between qualitative interview results and neuroimaging results, both centering around the idea that charitable bequest contemplation involves visualized autobiography.

New experiment

- 36 participants (20 female, 16 male)
- Attempted increasing realism of decision-making
- Now comparing different types of BEQUEST decision (not bequest giving v. current giving)

In the next experiment, we attempted to take a different approach to analyzing the neural correlates of charitable bequest decision-making. First, we attempted to increase the realism of the decision-making context and second, we compared not different types of charitable giving, but different types of bequest recipients. In this case we were not comparing bequest giving to current giving or volunteering, but instead we were comparing making bequest gifts to charitable organizations with making bequest gifts to family members or making bequests gifts to friends.

At the end of this session, a legally valid last will and testament will be mailed to you at no charge. To help you design your plan, we need to ask about some of your desires and preferences...

(in varied order) About what percentage of your estate would you like to go to any charities?... friends who are not family members?... family members?

Are there any specific personal property items you would like to leave to any charities? ...friends who are not family members? ...family members?

Would you like to leave any specific dollar amount cash gifts (e.g., $250) to any charities? ...friends who are not family members? ....family members?

The above text shows what was presented to the participants, across a large number of slides, in this experiment. To begin with, the participants were informed that at the end of the session a legally valid last Will and Testament would be mailed to them at no charge, and that the questions they were about to respond to would assist in designing that plan. The idea here was to make the decisions as real as possible, given the context that the participants were in a scanner during the time that the questions were being asked.

After this introduction, participants were asked about

their preferences for leaving assets to charities, friends who were not family members, and family members. This was asked about residual (i.e., percentage) gifts, about specific personal property items, and about specific cash gifts. Participants responded to these questions by either selecting a level of agreement or, in the case of the percentage question, using a slider bar to select the precise percentage intended for each separate recipient group. In this section questions were asked not about individual recipients, but only about recipient groups. Consequently, we had a smaller number of repetitions with this analysis as compared with the previous analysis. All together, we had a total of nine different responses from 36 participants to use in this analysis.

As compared with charitable bequest decisions, bequests to friends and family more heavily involve

1. **Emotion** (mid/posterior cingulate cortex; insula)
   See Maddock, Garrett & Buonocore, 2003
2. **Memory** (hippocampus)

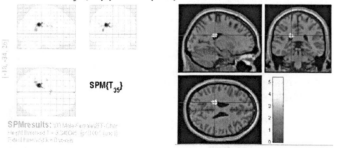

This difference was stronger for females than males. As compared with resting state, bequest decisions more strongly activated lingual gyrus and precuneus, in addition to a wide range of regions associated with reading, cognition and button pressing.

The preceding image shows the areas of greatest differential activation comparing charitable bequest decisions with bequest decisions to friends and family members. The results show a greater activation in areas associated with emotion and memory during bequest decision making related to family members and friends than during bequest decision-making processes related to charitable recipients. Activation was seen in the mid-cingulate cortex and posterior cingulate cortex as well as the insula. These regions have previously been associated with emotional responses. Additionally, greater activation in the hippocampus, which, as discussed before, has been associated repeatedly with memory and recall, was associated with bequest decision-making involving friends or family members as compared with bequest decision making involving charitable beneficiaries.

Although this finding is unsurprising, it provides some neurological evidence that bequest decisions involving friends and family members naturally engage much more substantial levels of emotion and memory than do bequest decisions involving charitable recipients. At this point we end the description of the results of the neuroimaging of bequest decision-making. For the remainder of this text, we will explore practical implications of the findings from the neuroimaging research.

Lower emotional and memory recall activation of charitable bequests (as compared with friends and family bequests) may help explain:

- Why charitable bequests are more rare than bequests to friends and family

- Why charitable bequests may be most compelling when memorializing a deceased loved one (i.e., connecting the emotion and memory of the loved one to the charity/cause)

The suggestion that contemplation of charitable bequests involves lower emotional and memory recall activity as compared with contemplation of bequests to friends and family is by no means shocking. However, understanding this reality may be part of the answer to the question of why charitable bequests are so much more rare than bequests to friends and family. The understanding of the relatively lower emotional and memory content of charitable bequest contemplation may also lead to the pragmatic consideration of attaching the charitable cause to the memory of a friend or family member. In other words, charitable bequests may be particularly compelling when they are memorializing a deceased loved one. In this way, the charitable cause, which we know generates relatively less emotion and memory, might be attached to the friend or family member, which we know generates a higher level of emotion and memory.

Bequest narratives

- Autobiographical connections with the charity
- Autobiographical connections with a deceased "loved one" memorialized via a charity

> "'[In my will] there's the Youth Hostel Association, first of all...it's **where my wife and I met**....Then there's the Ramblers' Association. **We've walked a lot** with the local group...Then Help the Aged, I've got to help the aged, **I am one**...The there's RNID because **I'm hard of hearing**...Then finally, the Cancer Research. **My father died of cancer** and so I have supported them ever since he died.'

Male, 89
married (Routley, 2011, p. 220-221)

So what then is the practical connection between the neuroimaging results and actual charitable bequest decision-making in the real world? I think it is instructive to look at some of the statements from the in-depth qualitative interviews completed by Dr. Routley in her dissertation. To make this distinction meaningful, notice in the above quote where one participant describes his reasons for including various charities that the description is permeated with references to autobiographical connections. These autobiographical connections may be with the charity itself, or they may be with a deceased loved one who was being memorialized through the support of the charity.

In this simple description of motivations by this respondent, we have the practical realization of the neuroimaging findings in both of our studies. We have both the connection of bequest decision-making with a person's life story and we have the use of memorialization to give to the charity as a way of honoring a friend or family member (thus, attaching the higher level of emotion and memory associated with the person to the relatively cold and impersonal corporate reality of the charity or charitable cause).

Bequest narratives

- Autobiographical connections with the charity
- Autobiographical connections with a deceased "loved one" memorialized via a charity

'The reason I selected Help the Aged...it was **after my mother died**...And I just thought – she'd been in a care home for probably three or four years. And I just wanted to help the elderly....I'd also support things like Cancer Research, because **people I've known have died**...An animal charity as well, **I had a couple of cats.'**

Female, 63
widowed
(Routley, 2011, p. 220-221)

As another example, the above quote also demonstrates the pragmatic reality associated with the neuroimaging results from both sets of research. Put into purely personal, qualitative, and descriptive terms, these narratives correspond with the findings from neuroimaging.

8 TESTING MESSAGES TO ENCOURAGE CHARITABLE BEQUESTS

Part III:
Testing
Messages
to
encourage
charitable
bequests

Testing new findings
from neuroimaging

Although we left behind neuroimaging results in the previous chapter, we will continue to explore results from other experiments in this chapter using a very different methodology. Again following the idea of triangulation, we want to take results from the psychological experimental literature and results from our neuroimaging to develop effective marketing interventions to change the attitudes and behaviors of potential donors. Ultimately, if the previous theoretical musings cannot generate marketing messages that impact behavior, then even if they might be of interest to academics, they won't help those who are practicing in planned giving.

And so, in this section we will attempt to test some interventions consistent with the findings from experimental psychology and neuroimaging to see if these have any effect on bequest giving intentions. And further, we will explore the relative effectiveness of several different messages on charitable bequest giving attitudes. This is the first place where we test behavioral interventions to see if there are practical implications of what we have so far been exploring only in the theoretical and neuroimaging realm. So let's get started.

The problem

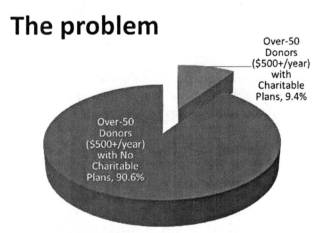

James, R. N., III. (2009). Health, wealth, and charitable estate planning: A longitudinal examination of testamentary charitable giving plans. Nonprofit and Voluntary Sector Quarterly, 38(6), 1026-1043.

The fundamental problem is the same that we have discussed throughout this text. The problem is that we have a gap. That gap is the difference between the percentage of people who engage in regular substantial charitable giving (which is a high percentage) and the percentage of people who engage in charitable bequest planning (which is a very low percentage).

Research Question: What messages reduce this gap?

Substantial donors during life	Substantial donors leaving any gift at death

So the bottom line, pragmatic question comes down to this simple idea: what can we do to reduce the gap? Specifically, what kind of marketing messages can we use that will most effectively help us to reduce this gap. Notice we are not concerned so much about how to get people to care more about charitable organizations. Although that's an important question, that's a question for fundraising and development in general the question of greatest interest for us is how do we reduce the gap between people who are willing to give currently and people who are willing to include a charity in their bequest planning.

The reason were not particularly concerned with how to develop an initial interest in charitable giving is that the gap is so massive that if we were able to simply close the gap between current giving and bequest giving participation, we would increase bequest giving participation by more than tenfold. Consequently, we are focused, not on how to make people like charities, but rather on how to eliminate the gap between their current giving behavior and their bequest giving behavior. (Perhaps at some point in the future if we are able to eliminate this gap in practice and achieve a more than tenfold increase in participation rates in charitable bequest giving, then we can turn our attention to the question of how we might best increase the level of connection to the charitable cause in general!)

The bequest giving gap is driven by two factors

We explore the impact of different messages on the first factor

The bequest gap is driven by two different factors. First is the issue of intention. In other words, "Do you plan to leave a charitable bequest?" Second is the issue of execution, that is, "Did you get the plan completed?" In this particular set of experiments, we looked only at the intention topic. Consequently, this was not exploring a complete solution. If we are able to change people's intentions such that they plan to complete a charitable bequest, that is a major step. But, a plan to complete a charitable bequest is, of course, not a completed charitable plan. But, it is a necessary prerequisite. There is no reason to explore how to encourage execution if the person has no intention to leave a charitable plan to begin with. This particular subcomponent of the gap is a necessary hurdle that we must be able to get over, but it is not a sufficient hurdle to produce the final results.

We test the current-bequest giving intention gap by comparing answers to these two questions with 2,500 survey respondents

"If you were asked in the next 3 months, what is the likelihood you might GIVE money to [organization]?"

v.

"If you signed a will in the next 3 months, what is the likelihood you might leave a BEQUEST gift to [organization]?"

We explored the current giving and bequest giving intention gap by asking two questions with regard to an extremely wide range of organizations. The first question is, "If you were asked in the next three months, what is the likelihood you might give money to... [the particular organization]?" We then compared the response to this question with the response to the question, "If you signed a will in the next three months, what is the likelihood you might leave a bequest gifts to ...[that same organization]?" These intention questions were the same intention questions that were used in the neuroimaging experiment. We used the same questions, except in this case we took them out of the scanner and put them out into the real world to see if we could alter the gap between current giving and bequest giving intentions.

In our first set of surveys, we tested a total of six different interventions using approximately 2,500 survey respondents. These interventions were tested using five different surveys, which included different combinations of these interventions. This resulted in about 500 participants for each survey type, because the 2,500 participants were randomly assigned to receive one of the five different surveys. Different surveys used different interventions and so we were able to compare different marketing interventions across the different randomly assigned groups.

Surveys responses were collected from an online survey service. Respondents were paid to complete the survey, and were required to be U.S. residents. Several mechanisms were used to ensure that the respondents were paying close attention to the questions. For example, the opening question was a simple, large font question of "How often do you take surveys" with five options. Above this question was a large paragraph of small font type which included, in the middle of the paragraph, special instructions regarding how to answer this question (by clicking the "no response" button), and a special phrase to enter into the accompanying text box. Those who did not click the correct button and enter the special phrase were kicked out of the survey and not allowed to take it. In total, approximately a third of those who started the survey were kicked out at this point for not paying attention to the details of the questions. There were also other hidden instructions included in the remaining parts of the survey.

Additionally, other mechanisms were used, such as employing minimum times before subsequent questions could be answered. These minimum time requirements meant that the participants could not move on to the next page until they had spent a sufficient amount of time contemplating the previous questions. These were all mechanisms attempting to make sure that the answers were thoughtful answers and did not come from respondents trying to rush through the survey.

Scored on a 1 to 100 point scale

"If you were asked in the next 3 months, what is the likelihood you might GIVE money to [organization]?"	0 – Absolutely no possibility under any circumstance 10 – Extremely highly unlikely 20 – Highly unlikely 30 – Somewhat unlikely 40 – Slightly more unlikely than likely 50 – 50-50 chance 60 – Slightly more likely than unlikely 70 – Somewhat likely 80 – Highly likely 90 – Extremely highly likely 100 – Absolutely certain without any possible doubt
v.	
"If you signed a will in the next 3 months, what is the likelihood you might leave a BEQUEST gift to [organization]?"	

One difference from the questions presented in the scanner was that participants had a much wide range of responses available in the online survey. In the scanner experiments, there were only four different levels of agreement. The online survey used 100 different levels of agreement, varying from 0 "absolutely no possibility under any circumstances" to 100 "absolutely certain without any possible doubt." Responses were provided by using a slider bar, which respondents could click and drag from 0 on the left to 100 on the right. The selected number was displayed above the bar, showing what level of agreement they had selected.

We explored results for 40 different organizations

American Cancer Society	The American Diabetes Association
National Cancer Coalition	Joslin Diabetes Center
Dana Farber Cancer Institute	UNICEF
MD Anderson Cancer Center	CARE
National Audubon Society	Guide Dogs for the Blind
Ducks Unlimited	Canine Companions for Independence
World Wildlife Fund	National Breast Cancer Foundation
Wildlife Conservation Society	Breast Cancer Research Foundation
AIDS Project Los Angeles	Susan G. Komen Breast Cancer
San Francisco AIDS Foundation	Foundation
Prevent Blindness America	The Alzheimer's Association
Foundation Fighting Blindness	The Alzheimer's Foundation
The American Humane Association	United Negro College Fund
American Society for Prevention of Cruelty to	American Indian College Fund
Animals	The American Heart Association
Big Brothers / Big Sisters of America	The American Lung Association
Boys and Girls Clubs of America	The Red Cross
YWCA	The United Way
YMCA	Goodwill Industries
Girl Scouts	The Salvation Army
Boy Scouts	Habitat for Humanity

In this experiment, we tested these results for 40 different large national charitable organizations which are listed above. As you will see later, when comparing across different groups, we often split organizations of the same type into two different groups in order to measure the effect of intervention types on each type of charity. Because of the number of different interventions used here, totaling six different types of interventions plus a control group, we were not able to apply all seven conditions to all 40 organizations. This would have made the survey length unwieldy. In its current form the typical respondent took about 35 minutes, on average, to complete the survey.

The survey was available online and all surveys were completed online. Respondents came from across the age spectrum of adults, with some fairly young and some quite old. In a later examination of the results we will separately examine responses from older adults, about whom we are particularly concerned when it comes to charitable bequest planning.

Prior to having the participants answer questions

related to bequest giving, they were required to answer a series of questions intended to induce mortality salience. The reason for this is that, in actual practice, bequest decisions are made in a context that has an extremely high level of personal mortality salience. In other words, the estate planning process typically does not happen instantaneously on the spur of the moment. Rather, it is an extended process that involves an extended period of contemplation of one's own personal mortality. Because that contemplation is inherent in the estate planning process, we wanted to duplicate the same decision-making environment, as much as possible, for our survey responses in order to increase the similarity with real-world decisions. Consequently, prior to answering our questions of interest, participants answered questions related to their preferences for personal funeral arrangements and burial options as well as their knowledge of estate planning related terms. Let's now turn to examining the results of the experiment.

Different organizations have different charitable bequest intention scores. But, **EVERY** organization has a **GAP** between giving intentions and bequest intentions

Organization	Bequest intention	Giving intention	Organization	Bequest intention	Giving intention
American Cancer Society	26.79	36.77	Wildlife Conservation Society	19.90	29.26
The Red Cross	25.93	41.12	Goodwill Industries	19.65	34.42
American Society for Prevention of Cruelty to Animals	24.18	33.77	Big Brothers / Big Sisters of America	19.47	30.49
Habitat for Humanity	24.01	34.90	The United Way	18.97	28.97
The American Heart Association	23.17	33.95	Joslin Diabetes Center	18.91	29.18
National Cancer Coalition	22.56	34.54	Canine Companions for Independence	18.90	29.67
Breast Cancer Research Foundation	22.53	33.93	Foundation Fighting Blindness	18.77	28.37
National Breast Cancer Foundation	22.43	33.48	AIDS Project Los Angeles	17.71	25.64
The American Humane Association	22.23	33.91	Prevent Blindness America	17.51	28.32
The Alzheimer's Foundation	21.40	32.00	San Francisco AIDS Foundation	17.39	25.49
Susan G. Komen Breast Cancer Foundation	21.39	29.22	National Audubon Society	17.33	24.24
Dana Farber Cancer Institute	21.13	29.63	YMCA	17.16	28.12
The American Diabetes Association	20.84	32.54	Boys and Girls Clubs of America	17.14	30.10
World Wildlife Fund	20.82	29.08	Girl Scouts	16.71	31.27
Guide Dogs for the Blind	20.80	31.46	YWCA	16.21	24.42
The Alzheimer's Association	20.80	31.86	American Indian College Fund	15.97	22.33
The American Lung Association	20.78	31.40	CARE	15.86	24.69
MD Anderson Cancer Center	20.59	30.53	Boy Scouts	14.51	23.56
UNICEF	20.37	32.31	United Negro College Fund	14.13	21.90
The Salvation Army	19.98	31.44	Ducks Unlimited	13.60	19.49

To begin with, we received results for bequest

intentions and gift intentions for all 40 charities from the respondents who received no marketing interventions. In the above chart, the column labeled "bequest intention," shows the average level of agreement with the bequest intention question. Similarly, the column labeled "giving intention" shows the average level of agreement with the giving intention question. (These are the scores using the 100-point agreement scale shown earlier.) Because this was an average response, it combined the typically large number of respondents giving a very low score, with the typically smaller number of respondents giving a high score for each particular charity.

As we look at these results for all 40 different organizations (here sorted from the highest bequest intention to the lowest bequest intention) we see that there were a wide range of scores associated with different organizations. Some charities had relatively high giving and bequest intentions among the people surveyed here. Some had relatively low giving and bequest intentions among the people surveyed here. However, there was one characteristic that every single organization shared in common. Whether they were ranked, on average, high or ranked, on average, low, they all shared the common experience of being ranked higher in giving intention than in bequest intention.

This confirms the idea that the presence of a gap between intention to give and intention to give through bequest is universal. It was true for cancer organizations. It was true for health organizations. It was true for international relief organizations. It was true for animal charities. It was true across the board. Thus, regardless of whether or not your particular charity of interest was on this list of 40 charities, we can say with pretty high confidence that your charity also has a gap between donors giving intentions and their bequest giving intentions. The gap is universal. Next we turn to examining interventions used in an attempt to close that gap.

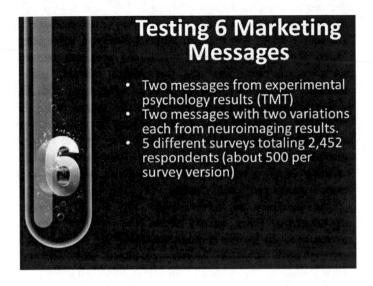

Testing 6 Marketing Messages

- Two messages from experimental psychology results (TMT)
- Two messages with two variations each from neuroimaging results.
- 5 different surveys totaling 2,452 respondents (about 500 per survey version)

We tested six different marketing messages. Two of these marketing messages were suggested by (or at least consistent with) the experimental psychology results and theory originating with "terror management theory." Two of the messages with two variations each were suggested by the findings from our neuroimaging results.

In total, there were five different surveys types used for this part of the study. The 2,452 respondents were relatively evenly distributed among the five survey types, resulting in about 500 respondents per survey version. As a side note, it is important to realize that although the interventions were consistent with these previous theories or findings, whether or not the intervention worked would not necessarily prove or disprove the previous theories or findings. Describing the connection simply recognizes the origin of the ideas for each intervention. Ultimately, the goal is to use the ideas suggested by the theories to identify effective marketing messages, and not to definitively support or contradict the previous theories or findings.

Message 1: Spendthrift heirs

Results from experimental psychology suggest that death reminders, such as estate planning, increase the desire for "symbolic immortality", i.e., the desire to leave a **lasting impact** on the world.

We play off of this desire, by sharing information detailing the *impermanence* of leaving a bequest to heirs.

Previous research from terror management theory suggests that, in the face of mortality reminders, we will be particularly interested in expressions of our self or our community that will live beyond us. We seek avenues that provide some level of symbolic immortality. This idea of symbolic immortality requires some sense of permanence. In other words, we want something that lasts. If it doesn't last, then it doesn't really provide significant psychological support against the unpleasant thought of our own disappearance and insignificance.

Playing off of this subconscious desire for permanence, we created an initial message intended to emphasize the impermanence of leaving money to noncharitable heirs. The idea was to present accurate statistical evidence about the rapidity with which inheritances are often spent as a way to motivate people to consider adding charitable beneficiaries along with gifts to heirs.

As expected, among those expressing a difference, people wanted more permanence for bequest gifts than current gifts by greater than 2 to 1 (915 v. 407) when asked this question:

> **With regard to the previous potential [or bequest] gifts, please state your preference as to how you would like the funds to be used**
> ○ Strongly prefer an immediate expenditure of all funds to advance the cause of the charity
> ○ Somewhat prefer an immediate expenditure of all funds to advance the cause of the charity
> ○ Slightly prefer an immediate expenditure of all funds to advance the cause of the charity
> ○ No Preference
> ○ Slightly prefer the establishment of a permanent fund generating perpetual income to advance the cause of the charity forever
> ○ Somewhat prefer the establishment of a permanent fund generating perpetual income to advance the cause of the charity forever
> ○ Strongly prefer the establishment of a permanent fund generating perpetual income to advance the cause of the charity forever

This intervention was based upon the theoretical assumption that people preferred to have permanence in their bequest giving. If people actually didn't prefer permanence, then the intervention, which emphasized the lack of permanence in noncharitable beneficiaries, might not make sense. To measure whether or not this assumption was valid, we asked people about their preferences for permanence in current charitable giving and bequest charitable giving.

The psychological experimental results from terror management theory would lead us to believe that people would like to have more permanence with a death-related gift than with a current gift. Indeed, this is what we found among those people who expressed a difference between the level of permanence. These individuals expressed a desire for greater permanence for bequest gifts by a margin of greater than 2 to 1. Of course, this does not mean that everyone holds the same opinion, but it does mean that among those who had a difference in preference, the dominant difference in preference was to prefer more permanence for bequest gifts.

Introduction to spendthrift heirs message

> A recent national U.S. study shows that 1/3 of all heirs receiving inheritances spend their entire inheritance within a few months. In addition, among all heirs, about half of the typical inheritance has been spent within 12 months.
>
> [Study Citation: Zagorsky, J. L. (2012). Do people save or spend their inheritances? Understanding what happens to inherited wealth. Journal of Family and Economic Issues]

Feeling somewhat confident about the differential underlying desire for permanence, let's move on to the actual intervention used in this case. We will refer to this as the "spendthrift heirs" intervention. First, participants were provided with data from a recent national study showing the substantial share of all heirs that spend all, or at least half, of their inheritance within just a few months. This is a published study and these are real results, so there was nothing a false about this part of the presentation. The results mentioned simply reflected the statistical reality of what happens to inherited money.

Spendthrift heirs message (continued)...

Which of the following factors do you think contributes to this extremely rapid expenditure of inherited funds in the U.S.?

	Strongly Agree	Agree	Neither Agree nor Disagree	Disagree	Strongly Disagree
Lack of financial planning	O	O	O	O	O
True financial need	O	O	O	O	O
Guilty feelings about receiving money from the death of a loved one	O	O	O	O	O
Rational, thoughtful financial decision-making	O	O	O	O	O
Treating inheritance like "fun money" or lottery winnings	O	O	O	O	O
Heirs who haven't worked hard to earn their own money	O	O	O	O	O
Expenditures on addictive substances	O	O	O	O	O

In addition to providing the initial information from the study, we wanted to make sure that participants really interacted with it. In other words, we wanted them to think about the implications of this information. We wanted them to really internalize the information presented here. In order to do that, we included a series of questions about their beliefs as to factors that contributed to the rapid expenditure of inherited funds in the United States.

Notice that some of the potential explanations also emphasized the potential negative impacts of leaving money to heirs, such as expenditure on addictive substances, heirs who haven't worked hard to earn their money, or treating inheritance like a lottery winning. All of these are intended to emphasize the impermanence and negative associations with traditional bequest recipients as compared to charitable bequest recipients.

Message 2:
Social norms

Results from experimental psychology suggest that death reminders (such as estate planning) increase allegiance to one's "in-group" and to "in-group" values and norms.

For the second set of interventions, we focused on the idea of social norms. Results from terror management theory experiments repeatedly confirm the idea that when faced with mortality reminders, people tend to attach more strongly to their in-group community and become more committed to the values of their in-group community. Using that knowledge, we created this intervention based on the premise that, because of mortality salience, people would become more attached to the in-group and in-group values (and consequently become less attached to any out-group or out-group values).

Because we didn't know anything about the particular in-groups of our respondents, other than that they were U.S. residents, we chose national characteristics as the in-group and contrasted that with other nation's characteristics as the out-group. It is useful to consider, before we get into this specific intervention, the intention behind its development. Simply put, we wanted to create the most extreme intervention we could. We wanted to, as strongly as possible, make the case for leaving a charitable bequest as an appropriate social norm.

The reason that we started with a strong intervention was because if we got no response from the most extreme intervention, then we could feel more comfortable with the idea that these factors simply weren't motivational. Once the extreme intervention has failed, it is most likely that softer versions of the same intervention would not produce anything either. On the other hand, if the extreme intervention did get a good response, then we could later test more reasonable (and practical) versions of the intervention. This is all a way to explain that the goal of the intervention was to intentionally present the most slanted information in order to see if it was possible to get any impact at all.

Introduction to social norms marketing message (underlying theme: you should leave a bequest gift, because it is the American thing to do)

> Unlike many foreign countries, it is quite common in the United States for people from the poorest to the richest to leave 5% or 10% of their estate to a charity when they die. We are interested in your opinion about this common American practice.

So for this intervention, we began with a preliminary statement intended to emphasize the idea that leaving a bequest gift is the American thing to do. In particular, we emphasized that it was a common American practice among those of all different economic levels. The purpose here was to emphasize that this behavior was an accepted norm which would apply to the survey respondents regardless of their economic level.

Social norms marketing message continued...

If you received an inheritance from a family member and later learned that the family member had left 10% of her estate to her favorite charity would you feel offended by her decision to leave this charitable bequest?

o Yes, definitely offended
o Maybe a little offended
o I don't know
o No, not really offended
o No, definitely not offended

Your answer will be added to this running total for the question:

Previous Answers

0.5% Yes, definitely offended
1.5% Maybe a little offended
2% I don't know
5% No, not really offended
91% No, definitely not offended

Posting these numbers is intended to suggest that everyone agrees that leaving a bequest gift is acceptable

The "American social norms" marketing message then continued by asking a survey question regarding whether or not the person would feel offended if they received an inheritance from a family member and later learned that the family member had left 10% of her estate to her favorite charity. There are two reasons for this phrasing. The first was to take the decision process and reverse it, so that the person considers being the recipient rather than the donor. It allows the person to fill the role of the beneficiary, giving moral consent to the transfer of funds to a charitable entity.

In this way we attempted to attach the positive social value, in this case not being greedy, to the desired behavior of leaving a charitable bequest. We attempted to attach a positive social norm to the behavior by reversing the decision context and then additionally, we broadcast group agreement with the social norm by publishing the "running total." This percentage distribution for the "running total" did not change during the course of the survey. Simply put, this was not a running total. This was a methodology used to suggest that essentially everyone agreed with leaving a bequest gift as an acceptable activity (or at least 96% of the sample agreed with that idea). The concept was to show that if the person believed the behavior was inappropriate, then they were clearly in a very small minority (i.e., not confirming to group social norms). Findings from terror management theory suggests that the last thing a person wants to experience following mortality salience is the sense that they are an outcast from their in-group. Note that the information in the inset box is a commentary and was not included in the original survey.

Social norms marketing message continued...

Unlike many foreign countries, it is quite common in the United States for people from the poorest to the richest to leave 5% or 10% of their estate to a charity when they die. We are interested in your opinion about this common American practice.

If you received an inheritance from a family member and later learned that the family member had left 5% of her estate to her favorite charity would you feel offended by her decision to leave this charitable bequest?

o Yes, definitely offended
o Maybe a little offended
o I don't know
o No, not really offended
o No, definitely not offended

> Here we just repeat the message with the 5% level instead of the 10% level

Your answer will be added to this running total for the question:
Previous Answers
0.2% Yes, definitely offended
1% Maybe a little offended
2% I don't know
5% No, not really offended
92% No, definitely not offended

The next page of the survey essentially repeated this same scenario but used the 5% charitable contribution level rather than the 10% charitable contribution level. This was just an attempt to repeat the information supporting charitable bequests as an accepted social norm. Once again, the "running total" demonstrated the vast acceptance of this behavior. Note again that the information in the inset box is a commentary and was not included in the original survey.

Social norms message: American Values

Unlike many foreign countries, it is quite common in the United States for people from the poorest to the richest to leave 5% or 10% of their estate to a charity when they die. We are interested in your opinion about this common American practice. Which of the following reasons might help to explain, in part, why Americans in particular are so likely to leave part of their estate to a charitable organization when they die?

	Strongly Agree	Agree	Neither Agree nor Disagree	Disagree	Strongly Disagree
unusual levels of American GENEROSITY	O	O	O	O	O
unusual levels of American INDEPENDENCE	O				
unusual levels of American RELIGIOUS BELIEF	O				
unusual levels of American INDUSTRIOUSNESS	O				
unusual levels of American SELF-RELIANCE	O	O	O	O	O
unusual levels of American EDUCATION	O	O	O	O	O
unusual levels of American FREEDOM	O	O	O	O	O

> The underlying message here is that you should leave a charitable bequest because it is the AMERICAN thing to do.

The last part of this intervention then asked a series of questions about the "established" social norm. This series of questions was intended to cause the participant to interact with and contemplate the idea that the behavior is not only a social norm, but is related to defining characteristics of the national identity. Consequently, the questions relate to other potentially positive defining characteristics of the national identity to strengthen the importance and in-group identity of the social norm.

To the extent that the social norm is identified not just with the in-group (in this case one's nation), but is identified with the cherished values which define the core characteristics of that in group, it makes rejection of the social norm (charitable bequest giving) a rejection of the ethical and moral norms of the national in-group. Note again that the information in the inset box is a commentary and was not included in the original survey.

The Results

> The first group had no marketing messages. So, this shows the "natural" levels of current giving intentions and bequest giving intentions.

Relationships with no marketing messages	Average Across All Orgs.	Avg. (Age 50+)	Survey Group	Org. Group
Giving intention	29.93	27.07	1	A&B
Bequest intention	19.63	12.75	1	A&B
Gap between giving intention and bequest intention	10.30	14.32	1	A&B
Difference in give-bequest gap with marketing message groups				
1: Data on rapid expenditure by heirs	-0.88	-2.93	2(a)	B
2: Charitable bequests as an American value	-1.50	-2.58	3(a)	B
(1) followed by (2)	-2.09	-5.47	2(b)	A
(2) followed by (1)	-2.47	-2.71	3(b)	A

The above table shows the results from the control group and the groups receiving the first two interventions. The top four rows report results from the control group. This group answered the giving and bequest intention questions without any marketing message interventions. Consequently, we will use these responses as our comparison point throughout later analyses.

The second column reports the average giving intention. The circled results show the average giving intention across all organizations and the average bequest intention across all organizations for the control group that received no marketing messages. As expected, we see that there was approximately a 10 point gap between giving intention and bequest intention.

The third column reports the same results, but limited only to those respondents who reported being age 50 or above. Perhaps a bit disturbingly, the giving-bequest intention gap was even greater for those who were age 50 and above. Thus, the problem appears worse for those whose decisions matter the most.

> **This gap is the problem we will focus on. Why will you give money, but not leave a bequest?**

	Average Across All Orgs.	Avg. (Age 50+)	Survey Group	Org. Group
Relationships with no marketing messages				
Giving intention	29.93	27.07	1	A&B
Bequest intention	19.63	12.75	1	A&B
Gap between giving intention and bequest intention	10.30	14.32	1	A&B
Difference in give-bequest gap with marketing message groups				
1: Data on rapid expenditure by heirs	-0.88	-2.93	2(a)	B
2: Charitable bequests as an American value	-1.50	-2.58	3(a)	B
(1) followed by (2)	-2.09	-5.47	2(b)	A
(2) followed by (1)	-2.47	-2.71	3(b)	A

The primary number we will focus on for this research project is the giving-bequest intention gap. Basically we want to know why people will give money, but not leave a bequest. More to the point, we want to know what can we do to reduce this tendency of people who are willing to give money, to be simultaneously

unwilling to leave a charitable bequest? We begin with the
reality that there is a substantial gap in the control group
that received no marketing messages. The gap is 10.3
points for the sample as a whole and 14.32 points for the
sample aged 50 and above. Notice this gap is not a
problem of people not liking the charity, which would
generate low numbers for both forms of support. Instead,
the problem is an aversion to one form of financial
support over another. The problem isn't that people don't
like the charitable organizations. Instead it's about the
ways in which people are willing to act in response to their
support of the charity. It is this gap that we will attempt to
reduce, or ideally even eliminate, with our marketing
messages.

> After stating their current giving
> intentions, this group read the
> spendthrift heirs marketing message, and
> was then asked about their bequest gift
> intentions for 20 charities.

Relationships with no marketing messages	Average Across All Orgs.	Avg. (Age 50+)	Survey Group	Org. Group
Giving intention	29.93	27.07	1	A&B
Bequest intention	19.63	12.75	1	A&B
Gap between giving intention and bequest intention	10.30	14.32	1	A&B
Difference in give-bequest gap with marketing message groups				
1: Data on rapid expenditure by heirs	-0.88	-2.93	2(a)	B
2: Charitable bequests as an American value	-1.50	-2.58	3(a)	B
(1) followed by (2)	-2.09	-5.47	2(b)	A
(2) followed by (1)	-2.47	-2.71	3(b)	A

Moving further down the table, we see the first
results from our marketing messages. This first group read
the spendthrift heirs marketing message and then were
asked about bequest gift intentions for 20 of the 40
charities. Notice in this table that the charities are broken
into two different groups, that is group A and group B.

When we divided charities into these two groups we attempted to keep representatives of all of the different charity types in both groups. Group A consisted of The American Cancer Society, National Audubon Society, The American Society for the Prevention of Cruelty to Animals, San Francisco Aids Foundation, Breast Cancer Research Foundation, Foundation Fighting Blindness, Boys and Girls Clubs of America, CARE, YWCA, The Alzheimer's Foundation of America, Dana Farber Cancer Institute, Wildlife Conservation Society, Guide Dogs for the Blind, American Indian College Fund, Habitat for Humanity, American Lung Association, Boy Scouts, The United Way, The Salvation Army, and Joslin Diabetes Center. Group B consisted of National Cancer Coalition, Ducks Unlimited, The American Humane Association, AIDS Project Los Angeles, National Breast Cancer Foundation, Prevent Blindness America, Big Brothers/ Big Sisters, UNICEF, YMCA, The Alzheimer's Association, MD Anderson Cancer Center, World Wildlife Fund, Canine Companions for Independence, United Negro College Fund, Susan G. Komen Breast Cancer Foundation, The American Heart Association, Girl Scouts, Goodwill Industries, The American Red Cross, and The American Diabetes Association.

The reason that we didn't test each intervention with every single charity is twofold. First, it would have dramatically expanded the size of the survey instrument, which already took on average 35 minutes. Second, it would not allow the ability to easily test the effect of stacking multiple marketing interventions.

Notice in this analysis, we are comparing the gap presented by the experimental group (which received marketing messages after the giving question but before the bequest question) to the gap presented by the control group (which received no marketing messages). We are thus comparing two separate groups, rather than making a before and after comparison of the same people. People have a hesitancy to change an initial response. Because of this attachment to personal consistency, we may not be able to see the impact of an intervention in a "before and after" analysis. This is true even when the intervention truly would have had an impact if the individual had not already committed to a response prior to being exposed to the intervention. This is the reason why in this analysis we are comparing different groups, rather than "before and after" changes.

The circled result shows us the difference in the gap between the experimental group (which received the marketing message) and the control group (which received no marketing message). In this first example, the gap was .88 points smaller for the experimental group (that receiving the spendthrift heirs marketing message) as compared with the control group (that received no marketing messages). In other words, the group that received the spendthrift heirs marketing message had a current giving-bequest giving intention gap of 9.42 points instead of 10.30 points.

This is modestly good news, in that it suggests this marketing message may have had some positive effect in reducing the gap between giving intention and bequest intention. One advantage of focusing on the intention gap, rather than the absolute level of bequest intention, is that it avoids the problem of having one group that just happened to be more charitably inclined than the other group, and mistaking this for an effect of the marketing intervention. Because we are focused on the gap (i.e., the difference between charitable giving intention and bequest giving intention) if one group was overall more charitable or less charitable, it wouldn't necessarily have any effect on the gap. The gap measures the difference between the desire to give by current giving and the desire to give by bequest giving.

Although the .88 reduction in the gap is a positive step, it is also relatively small. Fortunately, some of our other results are more encouraging.

> **But, notice that the spendthrift heirs message more strongly impacted older respondents.**

Relationships with no marketing messages	Average Across All Orgs.	Avg. (Age 50+)	Survey Group	Org. Group
Giving intention	29.93	27.07	1	A&B
Bequest intention	19.63	12.75	1	A&B
Gap between giving intention and bequest intention	10.30	14.32	1	A&B
Difference in give-bequest gap with marketing message groups				
1: Data on rapid expenditure by heirs	-0.88	-2.93	2(a)	B
2: Charitable bequests as an American value	-1.50	-2.56	3(a)	B
(1) followed by (2)	-2.09	-5.47	2(b)	A
(2) followed by (1)	-2.47	-2.71	3(b)	A

The result circled above indicates that the "spendthrift heirs" message had a much greater effect on older respondents. It might be that the older respondents were thinking of the spendthrift heirs as spending the respondents' money, where the younger respondents might have been thinking about being a recipient of a bequest transfer. It may also be that the younger respondents were more likely to see immediate expenditure as a completely appropriate use of an inheritance.

Next we turn to the third group, which did not begin by receiving the spendthrift heirs message, but instead began by receiving the "American social norms" message. Notice also that this third group answered questions about the same set of organizations as the second group did.

> The gap was smaller for the group receiving the "American social norms" message than for the group that had received the "spendthrift heirs" message".

Relationships with no marketing messages	Average Across All Orgs.	Avg. (Age 50+)	Survey Group	Org. Group
Giving intention	29.93	27.07	1	A&B
Bequest intention	19.63	12.75	1	A&B
Gap between giving intention and bequest intention	10.30	14.32	1	A&B
Difference in give-bequest gap with marketing message groups				
1: Data on rapid expenditure by heirs	-0.88	-2.93	2(a)	B
2: Charitable bequests as an American value	-1.50	-2.58	3(a)	B
(1) followed by (2)	-2.09	-5.47	2(b)	A
(2) followed by (1)	-2.47	-2.71	3(b)	A

According to the circled results, for the sample as a whole, the "American social norms" message appears to have been more powerful in reducing the gap than the spendthrift heirs message. Notice, however, that this was not the case for older adults. For older adults, both messages were relatively similar in their impact, although the "spendthrift heirs" message was slightly more powerful in reducing the gap.

This emphasizes the importance of age appropriate messaging in this field. Ultimately, what we can say from these first two results is that both messages appear to have had some impact in reducing the gap. However, the spendthrift heirs message was primarily effective for an older audience, not a younger audience.

As an additional way to compare the impact of these messages, we then gave the second message to the group that already had received the first message and vice-versa. After receiving both sets of marketing messages the respondents in both groups then answered bequest questions regarding the 20 remaining charities. It is important to note that none of the marketing messages were delivered until after the current giving questions were asked. These marketing messages were given between the time that the current giving questions were asked and the time that the bequest giving intention questions were asked. Thus, the gap is never reduced by the intervention changing the current giving intentions, but only by the intervention changing the bequest giving intentions

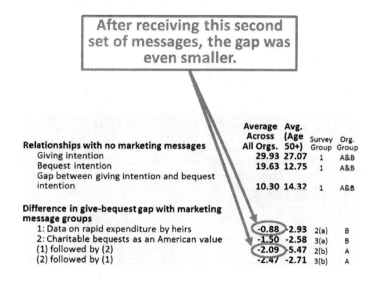

	Average Across All Orgs.	Avg. (Age 50+)	Survey Group	Org. Group
Relationships with no marketing messages				
Giving intention	29.93	27.07	1	A&B
Bequest intention	19.63	12.75	1	A&B
Gap between giving intention and bequest intention	10.30	14.32	1	A&B
Difference in give-bequest gap with marketing message groups				
1: Data on rapid expenditure by heirs	-0.88	-2.93	2(a)	B
2: Charitable bequests as an American value	-1.50	-2.58	3(a)	B
(1) followed by (2)	-2.09	5.47	2(b)	A
(2) followed by (1)	-2.47	-2.71	3(b)	A

After receiving this second set of messages, the gap was also smaller.

Relationships with no marketing messages	Average Across All Orgs.	Avg. (Age 50+)	Survey Group	Org. Group
Giving intention	29.93	27.07	1	A&B
Bequest intention	19.63	12.75	1	A&B
Gap between giving intention and bequest intention	10.30	14.32	1	A&B
Difference in give-bequest gap with marketing message groups				
1: Data on rapid expenditure by heirs	-0.88	-2.93	2(a)	B
2: Charitable bequests as an American value	-1.50	-2.58	3(a)	B
(1) followed by (2)	-2.09	-5.47	2(b)	A
(2) followed by (1)	-2.47	-2.71	3(b)	A

So, in both cases, adding the second message improved results
(although tested with a new set of charitable organizations)

Relationships with no marketing messages	Average Across All Orgs.	Avg. (Age 50+)	Survey Group	Org. Group
Giving intention	29.93	27.07	1	A&B
Bequest intention	19.63	12.75	1	A&B
Gap between giving intention and bequest intention	10.30	14.32	1	A&B
Difference in give-bequest gap with marketing message groups				
1: Data on rapid expenditure by heirs	-0.88	-2.93	2(a)	B
2: Charitable bequests as an American value	-1.50	-2.58	3(a)	B
(1) followed by (2)	-2.09	-5.47	2(b)	A
(2) followed by (1)	-2.47	-2.71	3(b)	A

The above results suggest that these messages were "stackable" in the sense that providing the second of the two messages in both cases seemed to provide an additional impact in reducing the giving-bequest intention gap. This was true when the "spendthrift heirs" message was added on to the "American social norms" message.

This was also true when the "American social norms" message was added on to the "spendthrift heirs" message. Both were true for the sample as a whole and for the sample limited to older adults.

Consequently, this suggests that these two interventions are complementary. We could theoretically emphasize both messages and get a bigger consequence than when we simply emphasized one. Nevertheless, the conclusions to be drawn from this are limited by the fact that the second set of questions referred to a different set of nonprofit organizations. Making a comparison across groups, it does appear that there was a larger impact from adding the "American social norms" message than from adding the "spendthrift heirs" message and that this was true in both the sample as a whole, and the older adult sample.

Marketing messages 3&4
Life stories

Our neuroimaging results with these questions suggests that bequest contemplation (as contrasted with current giving) engages "visualized autobiography" regions

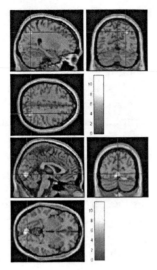

James, R. N., III & O'Boyle, M. (in press) Charitable estate planning as visualized autobiography: An fMRI study of its neural correlates. Nonprofit and Voluntary Sector Quarterly.

For the next set of interventions we will look at "life story" messages with a visual component. The previous neuroimaging results were consistent with the hypothesis that bequest contemplation particularly engages visualized autobiography regions as compared with current giving contemplation. Following from this finding, we use marketing messages taken from the Leave a Legacy® campaign about the life stories of deceased donors and how those deceased donors are continuing to make an impact consistent with their life story many years after the death of the donor. The text is taken from the Leave a Legacy® campaign, however, the images are not those used with the campaign materials. We used these different images in part because we also modified the text of the Leave a Legacy® campaign stories for an additional variation where the stories were of currently living donors and their plans for making an impact in the future through planned charitable bequest giving, and we wanted the images to be easily interchangeable with both types of stories.

Message Type 3: Life stories of deceased donors
Text from the Leave a Legacy® campaign

School janitor Lester Holmes died in 1992.

After school today, he'll help an 8-year-old understand math.

Lester never finished school, but he learned a lot mopping classroom floors. "You kids can be anything you want," he'd say. Lester wasn't rich, but because he included a gift to support the school's tutoring program in his will, things will add up for a few more students. Include your favorite cause in your will or estate plan.

The above is an example of the life stories of deceased donors used in this survey.

Message Type 4: Life stories of living donors
Modified text from Leave a Legacy®

School janitor Lester Holmes signed his will today.

One day, his charitable bequest gift will help an 8-year-old understand math.

Different groups saw different ads, but no one saw both versions of the same ad.

Lester never finished school, but he learned a lot mopping classroom floors. "You kids can be anything you want," he'd say. Lester wasn't rich, but because he included a gift to support the school's tutoring program in his will, things will add up for a few more students. Include your favorite cause in your will or estate plan.

The above shows an example modification of the original text to generate life stories of living donors who have planned to leave a charitable bequest. Notice that the text is kept as close to the original as possible while changing the story from that of a decedent to that of a living planner. Also note that different groups saw different ads, but no one saw the same add in both versions (i.e., no one saw the same add in both its "living donor" and "deceased donor" formats).

The following images show the exact ads that were used in these tests. The group exposed to the life stories of deceased donors first would have seen the ads shown in the left column (following the deceased donor ad shown above). The group exposed to the life stories of living donors first would have seen the ads displayed in the right column (following the living planned bequest donor shown above). The bequest questions for the first 20 charities were asked after the first set of ads (either living or deceased donors) and then the questions related to the remaining 20 charities were asked after the remaining ads had been displayed.

INSIDE THE MIND OF THE BEQUEST DONOR

Symphony patron Maria Sanchez died in 1984

On Friday night, she'll present a program of Bach, Brahms and Beethoven

A lifelong music lover, Maria never missed a classical concert. The works of the old masters made her heart soar. Other hearts will soar because Maria included a bequest to the symphony in her will. Thanks to Maria, her beloved orchestra won't miss a beat. Include your favorite cause in your will or estate plan.

Symphony patron Maria Sanchez signed her will today

Even after she is gone, she will still be presenting programs of Bach and Brahms

A lifelong music lover, Maria never misses a classical concert. The works of the old masters make her heart soar. Other hearts will soar because Maria included a bequest to the symphony in her will. Thanks to Maria, her beloved orchestra won't miss a beat. Include your favorite cause in your will or estate plan.

Ralph Peterson signed his will today instead of visiting his favorite fishing hole.

His charitable bequest gift will, one day, release hundreds of bluegills into its waters.

Ralph is happiest sitting next to a pond with his grandkids, waiting for the bluegills to bite. To keep the pond stocked for his great-grandchildren, he included a bequest to a local conservation organization in his will. Thanks to Ralph, the fish will still be biting for generations to come. Include your favorite cause in your will or estate plan.

Ralph Peterson was buried beside his favorite fishing hole in 1997.

This Saturday at 2 p.m., he'll release a hundred bluegills into its waters.

Ralph was happiest sitting next to a pond with his grandkids, waiting for the bluegills to bite. To keep the pond stocked for his great-grandchildren, he included a bequest to a local conservation organization in his will. Thanks to Ralph, the fish are still biting. Include your favorite cause in your will or estate plan.

Coach Jim Bindley included a charitable gift in his will.

Even after he is gone, he'll still be sending four kids to football camp every summer

Jim loves to coach, not just because he loves football, but because he believes sports can teach important lessons. To continue those lessons, Jim placed a bequest to fund camp scholarships in his will. Thanks to Coach Bindley, a few more kids will reach their goals. Include your favorite cause in your will or estate plan.

Coach Jim Bindley died in 2002.

This summer, he'll send four kids to football camp

Jim loved to coach, not just because he loved football, but because he believed sports could teach important lessons. To continue those lessons, Jim placed a bequest to fund camp scholarships in his will. Thanks to Coach Bindley, a few more kids will reach their goals. Include your favorite cause in your will or estate plan.

Dr. Marjorie Chun included a charitable gift in her will.

After she is gone, she'll build a chapel in the hospital where she worked.

Dr. Chun practices the science of medicine, but she is also a woman of faith. To help her hospital treat body and soul, she will fund a new chapel with a gift from her estate plan. Thanks to Dr. Chun, patients and their families will one day have a place to seek peace. Include your favorite cause in your will or estate plan.

Dr. Marjorie Chun died in 2000.

This fall, she'll build a chapel in the hospital where she worked.

Dr. Chun practiced the science of medicine, but she was also a woman of faith. To help her hospital treat body and soul, she funded the new chapel with a gift from her estate plan. Thanks to Dr. Chun, patients and their families will have a place to seek peace. Include your favorite cause in your will or estate plan.

Ads were on the screen for a fixed duration followed by questions about the ad, such as:

What was the name of the person described in the previous advertisement?
o Jim Bindley
o Dominic Mason
o Ralph Peterson
o Lester Holmes

What type of charity did the previous described gift benefit?
o Symphony
o Choir
o Ballet
o Opera
o Theatre

	Strongly Agree	Agree	Neither Agree nor Disagree	Disagree	Strongly Disagree
Inspirational	O	O	O	O	O
Makes you think	O	O	O	O	O
Boring	O	O	O	O	O
Inaccurate	O	O	O	O	O

In order to make sure that individuals were paying attention to the content of the advertisements each advertisement was followed by different types of questions. These questions asked about the content of the ad. Some required the participant to remember the text content. Others asked the participants' opinions regarding the characteristics of the advertisement. The primary goal of these questions was to encourage participants to closely examine the advertisements, knowing that they would later be asked questions regarding the content.

> ## The gap for this group was lower than for any combination of the previous marketing messages

Relationships with no interventions	Average Across All Orgs.	Avg. (Age 50+)	Survey Group	Org. Group
Giving intention	29.93	27.07	1	A&B
Bequest intention	19.63	12.75	1	A&B
Gap between giving intention and bequest intention	10.30	14.32	1	A&B
Difference in give-bequest gap with intervention groups				
1: Data on rapid expenditure by heirs	-0.88	-2.93	2(a)	B
2: Charitable bequests as an American value	-1.50	-2.58	3(a)	B
(1) followed by (2)	-2.09	-5.47	2(b)	A
(2) followed by (1)	-2.47	-2.71	3(b)	A
3: Stories of deceased bequest donors making an impact	-5.29	-7.65	4(a)	A
4: Stories of living bequest planners future impact	-3.52	-6.71	5(a)	B
(3) followed by (4)	-5.31	-7.93	4(b)	B
(4) followed by (3)	-3.31	-6.62	5(b)	A

The above table displays these results in addition to the one's seen from the previous interventions. The results from the deceased bequest donor stories show an impact greater than any seen for the previous two interventions, either alone or combined.

> ## When we then added some "live donor stories" ads for this group, the gap didn't change much.

Relationships with no interventions	Average Across All Orgs.	Avg. (Age 50+)	Survey Group	Org. Group
Giving intention	29.93	27.07	1	A&B
Bequest intention	19.63	12.75	1	A&B
Gap between giving intention and bequest intention	10.30	14.32	1	A&B
Difference in give-bequest gap with intervention groups				
1: Data on rapid expenditure by heirs	-0.88	-2.93	2(a)	B
2: Charitable bequests as an American value	-1.50	-2.58	3(a)	B
(1) followed by (2)	-2.09	-5.47	2(b)	A
(2) followed by (1)	-2.47	-2.71	3(b)	A
3: Stories of deceased bequest donors making an impact	-5.29	-7.65	4(a)	A
4: Stories of living bequest planners future impact	-3.52	-6.71	5(a)	B
(3) followed by (4)	-5.31	-7.93	4(b)	B
(4) followed by (3)	-3.31	-6.62	5(b)	A

In the results circled above, we can see that adding living bequest donor stories to deceased bequest donor stories did not appreciably change the impact on the giving-bequest intention gap. This same result appears relatively consistent throughout all of the applications of these "life story" interventions, even when the sequence of nonprofit groups was switched. Taken together, this suggests that the two types of "life story" messages are not "stackable" in the sense that adding one type to another does not provide an additional large boost. Rather, the messages appear to be largely interchangeable.

> The final group got the "living donor story" ads. These also resulted in a smaller gap than for any non-story message combinations.

	Average Across All Orgs.	Avg. (Age 50+)	Survey Group	Org. Group
Relationships with no interventions				
Giving intention	29.93	27.07	1	A&B
Bequest intention	19.63	12.75	1	A&B
Gap between giving intention and bequest intention	10.30	14.32	1	A&B
Difference in give-bequest gap with intervention groups				
1: Data on rapid expenditure by heirs	-0.88	-2.93	2(a)	B
2: Charitable bequests as an American value	-1.50	-2.58	3(a)	B
(1) followed by (2)	-2.09	-5.47	2(b)	A
(2) followed by (1)	-2.47	-2.71	3(b)	A
3: Stories of deceased bequest donors making an impact	-5.29	-7.65	4(a)	A
4: Stories of living bequest planners future impact	-3.52	-6.71	5(a)	B
(3) followed by (4)	-5.31	-7.93	4(b)	B
(4) followed by (3)	-3.31	-6.62	5(b)	A

> **When we then added some "deceased donor stories" ads for this group, and then asked about a different set of charities, the gap didn't change much.**

Relationships with no interventions	Across All Orgs.	(Age 50+)	Survey Group	Org. Group
Giving intention	29.93	27.07	1	A&B
Bequest intention	19.63	12.75	1	A&B
Gap between giving intention and bequest intention	10.30	14.32	1	A&B
Difference in give-bequest gap with intervention groups				
1: Data on rapid expenditure by heirs	-0.88	-2.93	2(a)	B
2: Charitable bequests as an American value	-1.50	-2.58	3(a)	B
(1) followed by (2)	-2.09	-5.47	2(b)	A
(2) followed by (1)	-2.47	-2.71	3(b)	A
3: Stories of deceased bequest donors making an impact	-5.29	-7.65	4(a)	A
4: Stories of living bequest planners future impact	-3.52	-6.71	5(a)	B
(3) followed by (4)	-5.31	-7.93	4(b)	B
(4) followed by (3)	-3.31	-6.62	5(b)	A

Overall, the donor story ads appeared much more effective than the other messages

Relationships with no interventions	Average Across All Orgs.	Avg. (Age 50+)	Survey Group	Org. Group
Giving intention	29.93	27.07	1	A&B
Bequest intention	19.63	12.75	1	A&B
Gap between giving intention and bequest intention	10.30	14.32	1	A&B
Difference in give-bequest gap with intervention groups				
1: Data on rapid expenditure by heirs	-0.88	-2.93	2(a)	B
2: Charitable bequests as an American value	-1.50	-2.58	3(a)	B
(1) followed by (2)	-2.09	-5.47	2(b)	A
(2) followed by (1)	-2.47	-2.71	3(b)	A
3: Stories of deceased bequest donors making an impact	-5.29	-7.65	4(a)	A
4: Stories of living bequest planners future impact	-3.52	-6.71	5(a)	B
(3) followed by (4)	-5.31	-7.93	4(b)	B
(4) followed by (3)	-3.31	-6.62	5(b)	A

In looking at all of the results from these tables, we can take from it that although all of the ads appear to have a positive impact in reducing the gap between giving intention and bequest intention, overall, the donor life story advertisements were more powerful than the other interventions. There is also some evidence that the stories of deceased donors may be slightly more powerful than the stories of living bequest planners. This remains to be determined, however, by future tests specifically intended to address this issue.

Our final set of results relate to tribute gifts, either memorial gifts for a deceased person or honoring gifts for a living person.

As compared with charitable bequest decisions, bequests to friends and family more heavily involve

1. **Emotion** (mid/posterior cingulate cortex; insula)
   See Maddock, Garrett & Buonocore, 2003
2. **Memory** (hippocampus)

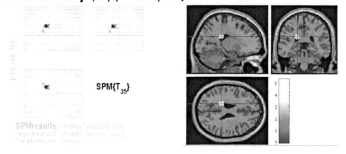

This difference was stronger for females than males. These results are not yet published and will be presented at academic conferences later this year.

This intervention was motivated by the neuroimaging

results showing that much greater emotion and memory activation attached to bequest decisions related to friends and family members than bequest decisions related to charities. This intervention is an attempt to attach the charity with the emotion and memory associated with a loved one. And further, it attempts to test whether or not such an attempted attachment can make an impact on stated intentions to leave a bequest gift.

Memorial or honoring gift reminders

Do you have a deceased friend or deceased family member who would have appreciated your support of a [ORGANIZATION TYPE] (such as the [EXAMPLE ORGANIZATIONS])?

If yes, please state your relationship to them and write at least 25 words describing their interest in or connection with this cause. If no, please write at least 25 words describing what you believe to be the typical characteristics of a person who supports this cause.

If you signed a will in the next 3 months, what is the likelihood you might leave a BEQUEST gift honoring a deceased friend or family member to each of the following organizations?

If asked in the next 3 months, what is the likelihood you might GIVE money honoring a deceased friend or family member to each of the following organizations?

Alternative versions replace "deceased friend or deceased family member" with "currently living friend or family member"

And "honoring a deceased friend or family member" with "honoring a living friend or family member"

The above slide shows the text of the questions for the memorial or honoring gift reminders. First, respondents were asked the question, "Do you have a deceased friend or deceased family member who would have appreciated your support of" a particular organization type, which was then followed by example organizations. For example, one question read, "Do you have a deceased friend or deceased family member who would have appreciated your support of a Cancer Research Organization (such as the National Cancer Coalition, the American Cancer Society, The MD Anderson Cancer Center, or the Dana Farber Cancer Institute)?" Other organizations types (and specific organizations) were a Wild Birds Preservation Organization (such as Ducks Unlimited or The National Audubon Society), an AIDS research and care organization (such as AIDS Project Los Angeles or San Francisco AIDS Foundation), an animal welfare organization (such as The American Humane Association or The American Society for the Prevention of Cruelty to Animals), a Youth-Related charitable organization (such as The Big Brothers/Big Sisters of America, Boys and Girls Clubs of America, YMCA, YWCA, Girl Scouts, or Boy Scouts), an Alzheimer's research and care organization (such as The Alzheimer's Association or The Alzheimer's Foundation of America), a blindness related nonprofit organization (such as Prevent Blindness America or Foundation Fighting Blindness), a diabetes research and treatment organization (such as The American Diabetes Association or The Joslin Diabetes Center), an International Relief charitable organization (such as UNICEF or CARE), a nonprofit organization supporting service dogs (such as Canine Companions for Independence or Guide Dogs for the Blind), a wildlife-focused nonprofit organization (such as the World Wildlife Fund or the Wildlife Conservation Society), and a breast cancer research organization (such as the National Breast Cancer Foundation, Breast Cancer Research Foundation, or Susan G. Komen Breast Cancer Foundation)

If the respondent answered, "yes" to this question, then they were asked to write at least 25 words describing the friend or family member and their friend or family member's interest in or connection with the cause. If the respondent answered, "no" to this question, they were asked to write 25 words on another issue. This was done primarily to equalize the workload between those who responded "yes" and "no" to the question, so as to not discourage "yes" answers. Following this reminder and writing requirement, both the current giving and bequest giving questions were asked again, although this time they were asked in the context of a gift honoring a deceased friend or family member.

For the alternate version of this intervention the deceased friend or deceased family member was replaced with a currently living friend or family member in order to compare the impact of tribute reminders for deceased associates with tribute reminders for living friends or family members.

Examining before and after changes within the same person (not group 1 v. group 2 as before)

ASKED EARLIER	ASKED AT END
"If you signed a will in the next 3 months, what is the likelihood you might leave a BEQUEST gift to [organization]?"	*"If you signed a will in the next 3 months, what is the likelihood you might leave a BEQUEST gift honoring a deceased friend or family member to [organization]?"*

We look at only those who answered "Yes" to having a friend/family member who would [would have] appreciated their support of the organization

Notice that here we are making a very different kind of comparison to those made with the previous interventions. Here we are comparing changes *within* the same individuals by comparing their answers before the intervention to their answers after the intervention. This may avoid the previously discussed problem of participants anchoring on their previous answer, because the second set of questions were slightly different. The second set of questions asked specifically about bequest gifts that honored or memorialized a friend or family member. Thus, the idea is that people would not feel that they were being inconsistent if they changed their earlier response because the questions themselves had changed.

Because we are looking at the same people (before v. after) we will be able to look directly at the change in their bequest giving intention rather than relying on examining only the gap between giving intention and bequest intention. (Remember that the gap analysis allowed us to protect against group differences in overall charitable inclinations towards nonprofits. We don't have to protect against this in the current analysis because we are comparing the same individuals' responses before and after the intervention.)

> **Here, the willingness to leave a bequest went up 8.55 points on the 100 point scale after the memorial reminder.**

	Total	Total (Age 50+)
Charitable bequest intentions		
Memorial v. Initial	8.55*** [n=1240]	10.00*** [n=191]
Memorial v. Initial (w/ preceding interventions)	7.98*** [n=3440]	9.03*** [n=578]
Honor living person v. Initial	7.43*** [n=1594]	12.40*** [n=175]
Honor living person v. Initial (w/ preceding interventions)	5.96*** [n=5250]	6.91*** [n=734]
Current charitable giving intentions		
Memorial v. Initial	-1.51 [n=1236]	-5.08* [n=191]
Memorial (w/preceding interventions) v. Initial	-0.02 [n=3440]	-1.47 [n=578]
Honor living person v. Initial	-5.71*** [n=1588]	-5.03* [175]
Honor living person (w/preceding interventions) v. Initial	-1.83*** [n=5250]	-4.92*** [n=734]

The above table of results shows the change in bequests and current giving intentions before and after each intervention. It compares stated intentions regarding the general bequest question before and regarding the narrower tribute bequest question after. In comparing the responses after the memorial reminder, we see a notable increase in charitable bequest intentions.

Note that this increase refers only to those who said "yes" to having a friend or family member who would have appreciated their support of the organization. The n= number refers to the total number of times a respondent said "yes" to having a friend or family member who would have appreciated his or her support for this category of nonprofit organization. The number circled above shows the impact of the memorial reminder among those who had received no other marketing interventions. Note that the impact here was even greater for the older adult sample (+10.00 points) than for the sample as a whole (+8.55 points). Given the relative importance of decisions made at older ages in generating charitable bequests, this is particularly encouraging for this type of intervention.

Technical side note: As a conceptual matter leaving a bequest gift that honors a deceased friend or family member is a subcategory of leaving a bequest gift for any purpose. Thus logically, we ought to see *less* willingness to leave a bequest gift for a narrowly defined purpose than to leave a bequest gift for any and every purpose imagined by the donor. This is not, however, how humans think. Most people do not naturally think of the ability to leave a bequest gift that honors a deceased friend or family member unless it is presented specifically as an alternative.

The next question is whether or not the improvements seen from this type of intervention still occurred among those individuals who had already seen a previous set of marketing messages. The second row of results provides the initial answer.

> We see a similar effect, even when other market messages had already been employed prior to the first response to the bequest question.

Charitable bequest intentions	Total	Total (Age 50+)
	8.55***	10.00***
Memorial v. Initial	[n=1240]	[n=191]
	7.98***	9.03***
Memorial v. Initial (w/ preceding interventions)	[n=3440]	[n=578]
	7.45***	12.40***
Honor living person v. Initial	[n=1594]	[n=175]
	5.96***	6.91***
Honor living person v. Initial (w/ preceding interventions)	[n=5250]	[n=734]
Current charitable giving intentions		
	-1.51	-5.08*
Memorial v. Initial	[n=1236]	[n=191]
	-0.02	-1.47
Memorial (w/preceding interventions) v. Initial	[n=3440]	[n=578]
	-5.71***	-5.03*
Honor living person v. Initial	[n=1588]	[175]
	-1.83***	-4.92***
Honor living person (w/preceding interventions) v. Initial	[n=5250]	[n=734]

These results suggest that the memorial bequest opportunity can be "stacked" with other marketing messages to achieve a high level of charitable bequest intentions. Note that in this second column, we are comparing the initial response to bequest intention questions. In the circled category, this initial bequest response occurred *after* the marketing interventions. This means that the initial comparison point had already been "bumped up" by the effects of the previously described marketing messages.

Even though the initial comparison point had already been impacted by the previous marketing messages, we still see a very strong – nearly identical – impact from the memorial reminders. This is quite an exciting result because it tells us that in the context of an extended marketing campaign we can stack the previous marketing messages and memorial reminders to achieve higher and higher levels of charitable bequest intentions. We next turn to the question of whether or not this same effect can be seen if we are honoring living family members as contrasted with deceased family members.

> It seems to be similarly effective whether honoring a deceased friend/family member or living friend/family member.

Charitable bequest intentions	Total	Total (Age 50+)
Memorial v. Initial	8.55*** [n=1240]	10.00*** [n=191]
Memorial v. Initial (w/ preceding interventions)	7.98*** [n=3440]	9.03*** [n=578]
Honor living person v. Initial	7.43*** [n=1594]	12.40** [n=175]
Honor living person v. Initial (w/ preceding interventions)	5.96*** [n=5250]	6.91*** [n=734]
Current charitable giving intentions		
Memorial v. Initial	-1.51 [n=1236]	-5.08* [n=191]
Memorial (w/preceding interventions) v. Initial	-0.02 [n=3440]	-1.47 [n=578]
Honor living person v. Initial	-5.71*** [n=1588]	-5.03* [175]
Honor living person (w/preceding interventions) v. Initial	-1.83*** [n=5250]	-4.92*** [n=734]

The next group of results comes from the same set of reminders, but this time directed towards living friends or family members. Taken together, the results appear to show that honoring a living person was roughly as effective as honoring a deceased person. For the group receiving no other marketing interventions, honoring a living person increased bequest intentions slightly less (+7.43 points) than did the memorial reminders (+8.55 points). However, among those over 50, the effect was stronger for living person reminders (+12.40) than for memorial reminders (+10.00). Among those who had received previous marketing messages, the effect was slightly weaker for honoring a living person than for memorial gifts in both age categories. To the extent that honoring a living person was a weaker intervention, the differences were quite small. However, given our mixed results here, it appears the two interventions were approximately equal in their effects.

> But, people do not want to make a current gift to honor a living or deceased friend or family member.

Charitable bequest intentions	Total	Total (Age 50+)
	8.55***	10.00***
Memorial v. Initial	[n=1240]	[n=191]
	7.98***	9.03***
Memorial v. Initial (w/ preceding interventions)	[n=3440]	[n=578]
	7.43***	12.40***
Honor living person v. Initial	[n=1594]	[n=175]
	5.96***	6.91***
Honor living person v. Initial (w/ preceding interventions)	[n=5250]	[n=734]
Current charitable giving intentions		
	1.51	-5.08*
Memorial v. Initial	[n=1236]	[n=191]
	-0.02	-1.47
Memorial (w/preceding interventions) v. Initial	[n=3440]	[n=578]
	-5.71***	-5.03*
Honor living person v. Initial	[n=1588]	[175]
	-1.83***	-4.92***
Honor living person (w/preceding Interventions) v. Initial	[n=5250]	[n=734]

In contrast with the universally strong positive results on charitable bequest intentions for tribute purposes, we had universally negative results from suggesting that people make a current gift to honor a living or deceased friend or family member. This does not suggest that the reminder reduces the desire to make current gifts for other purposes, only that individuals are not interested in making current gifts for the purpose of honoring a living or deceased friend or family member. So the identical intervention works exceedingly well for bequest giving and exceedingly poorly for current giving.

This is once again another example of how bequest giving is fundamentally a different animal than current giving. This might be explained by cultural differences that support the use of independently created bequest gifts for these kinds of tributes, but expect that current gifts for tribute purposes be initiated by someone else (such as at the request of a close family member of the decedent or honoree).

Stacking earlier interventions with memorial/honoring reminders
(group effects + within-person changes)

giving v. bequest gap in the group with no interventions

v.

initial giving v. final bequest gap in groups exposed to interventions AND who responded "Yes" to having a friend/family member who would [would have] appreciated their support of the organization

The last analysis of this section looks at the possibility of stacking a series of interventions together. In particular, we want to look at the combined effects of first applying the marketing message interventions (which apply to charitable bequest decision-making in general) and then adding to this general marketing intervention the reminder of a friend or family member who would appreciate (or would have appreciated) the support and asking about interest in a tribute bequest gift. Learning whether or not messages can be stacked is important. If a series of positive results from different messages cannot be stacked, it means we have multiple avenues to get the same result. Although it is helpful to know that we have multiple avenues to get to the same result, it is not as powerful as learning that certain techniques, when placed together, can have an even larger effect than when used alone. If techniques can be successfully stacked, then we can get even closer to eliminating the gap between bequest gift intentions and current gift intentions. But if the techniques cannot be stacked then we simply have different ways to produce approximately the same reduction in the gap.

However, in this case, examining the combined effect is made more difficult because we are combining two types of measurements. On the one hand, we are examining a comparison across groups (inter-person differences). The initial marketing interventions compare differences between a group that had received the marketing intervention and a group that had not received the intervention. On the other hand, the tribute reminders compare individuals' prior answers with their subsequent answers. This examines within-person changes (intra-person differences) rather than cross group differences (inter-person differences).

To combine both of these interventions requires comparing the tribute bequest gift intentions with the current giving intentions acquired prior to either the marketing interventions or the tribute reminder. This is the gap between pre-existing current giving intentions and ultimate bequest giving intentions after two marketing interventions and the tribute reminder were applied. Finally, we compare that gap to the giving-bequest gap that existed for the group where no interventions were applied.

Now we combine the effects of the marketing messages with memorial/honoring giving.

Interventions	Avg. gap	American Cancer Society	National Cancer Coalition	Dana Farber Cancer Institute	MD Anderson Cancer Center	National Audubon Society	Ducks Unlimited	AIDS Project Los Angeles	San Francisco AIDS Found.
None (Baseline giving-bequest gap)	8.66	9.98	11.98	8.50	9.94	6.91	5.89	7.93	8.11
Δ Memorial alone	-6.20	-5.63 [216/486]	-2.95 [216/486]	-6.05 [216/486]	-6.79 [216/486]	-10.7 [58/473]	-17.1 [58/473]	-16.08 [54/466]	-24.96 [54/466]
Δ Memorial + info 1&2	-7.59	-10.07 [230/488]	-6.55 [230/488]	-11.11 [230/488]	-9.33 [230/488]	-8.18 [55/484]	-0.25 [55/484]	-5.62 [52/478]	-6.57 [52/478]
Δ Honor Living Person + info 1 & 2	-7.84	-6.78 [275/476]	-11.36 [275/476]	-9.08 [275/476]	-9.47 [275/476]	-7.91 [90/473]	-4.11 [90/473]	-4.72 [78/469]	-11.19 [78/469]

The ultimate goal of this section is to examine the combined effects of the marketing messages with the opportunity to engage in memorial or honoring bequest giving.

And we ask, for those who answered "yes" to the friend/family question AND received the marketing messages, did the giving-bequest gap completely disappear?

Interventions	Avg. gap	American Cancer Society	National Cancer Coalition	Dana Farber Cancer Institute	MD Anderson Cancer Center	National Audubon Society	Ducks Unlimited	AIDS Project Los Angeles	San Francisco AIDS Found.
None (Baseline giving-bequest gap)	8.66	9.98	11.98	8.50	9.94	6.91	5.89	7.93	8.11
Δ Memorial alone	-6.20	-5.63 [216/486]	-2.95 [216/486]	-6.05 [216/486]	-6.79 [216/486]	-10.7 [58/473]	-17.1 [58/473]	-16.08 [54/466]	-24.96 [54/466]
Δ Memorial + info 1&2	-7.59	-10.07 [230/488]	-6.55 [230/488]	-11.11 [230/488]	-9.33 [230/488]	-8.18 [55/484]	-0.25 [55/484]	-5.62 [52/478]	-6.57 [52/478]
Δ Honor Living Person + info 1 & 2	-7.84	-6.78 [275/476]	-11.36 [275/476]	-9.08 [275/476]	-9.47 [275/476]	-7.91 [90/473]	-4.11 [90/473]	-4.72 [78/469]	-11.19 [78/469]

Specifically, we want to know for the group that answered "yes" to having a friend or family member (either alive or deceased) who would have appreciated their support of a particular type of organization, whether or not the giving-bequest gap would disappear completely. Note, this would not mean the gap would disappear completely for all individuals. Instead, it tests whether or not the gap disappears for those individuals agreeing that they have a friend or family member who would appreciate (or would have appreciated) their support for the organization.

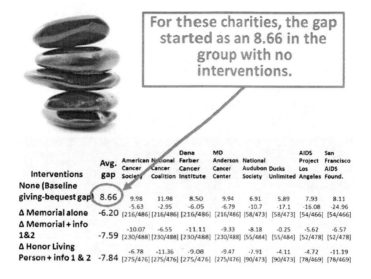

For these charities, the gap started as an 8.66 in the group with no interventions.

Interventions	Avg. gap	American Cancer Society	National Cancer Coalition	Dana Farber Cancer Institute	MD Anderson Cancer Center	National Audubon Society	Ducks Unlimited	AIDS Project Los Angeles	San Francisco AIDS Found.
None (Baseline giving-bequest gap)	8.66	9.98	11.98	8.50	9.94	6.91	5.89	7.93	8.11
Δ Memorial alone	-6.20	-5.63 [216/486]	-2.95 [216/486]	-6.05 [216/486]	-6.79 [216/486]	-10.7 [58/473]	-17.1 [58/473]	-16.08 [54/466]	-24.96 [54/466]
Δ Memorial + info 1&2	-7.59	-10.07 [230/488]	-6.55 [230/488]	-11.11 [230/488]	-9.33 [230/488]	-8.18 [55/484]	-0.25 [55/484]	-5.62 [52/478]	-6.57 [52/478]
Δ Honor Living Person + info 1 & 2	-7.84	-6.78 [275/476]	-11.36 [275/476]	-9.08 [275/476]	-9.47 [275/476]	-7.91 [90/473]	-4.11 [90/473]	-4.72 [78/469]	-11.19 [78/469]

Because of the complexity of stacking these kinds of interventions, we were not able to use every single combination of interventions with every nonprofit organization. Consequently, different intervention combinations were used for different organizations. The tables in this section show which organizations were used for the different types of interventions. As a result, the baseline giving-bequest intention gap will differ across organizations because the individual organizations examined will differ.

In our first set of results, the above circle highlights that this group of charities had a combined giving-bequest intention gap that averaged 8.66 when there were no interventions. The table above also shows these gaps for each individual organization involved. This is the baseline gap, as it is the gap when no marketing interventions and no memorial or honoring reminders were given.

> Among those given only the memorial bequest opportunity (who said yes to the friend/family question) the gap dropped by 6.2 points. So, it didn't completely disappear.

Interventions	Avg. gap	American Cancer Society	National Cancer Coalition	Dana Farber Cancer Institute	MD Anderson Cancer Center	National Audubon Society	Ducks Unlimited	AIDS Project Los Angeles	San Francisco AIDS Found.
None (Baseline giving-bequest gap)	8.66	9.03	11.98	8.50	9.94	6.91	5.89	7.93	8.11
Δ Memorial alone	-6.20	-5.63 [216/486]	-2.95 [216/486]	-6.05 [216/486]	-6.79 [216/486]	-10.7 [58/473]	-17.1 [58/473]	-16.08 [54/466]	-24.96 [54/466]
Δ Memorial + info 1&2	-7.59	-10.07 [230/488]	-6.55 [230/488]	-11.11 [230/488]	-9.33 [230/488]	-8.18 [55/484]	-0.25 [55/484]	-5.62 [52/478]	-6.57 [52/478]
Δ Honor Living Person + info 1 & 2	-7.84	-6.78 [275/476]	-11.36 [275/476]	-9.08 [275/476]	-9.47 [275/476]	-7.91 [90/473]	-4.11 [90/473]	-4.72 [78/469]	-11.19 [78/469]

The next row down reports the impact of the memorial reminders on the giving-bequest gap for those individuals who received no other marketing interventions. For these individuals, the giving-bequest gap dropped by 6.20 points. This was a substantial drop, but did not completely eliminate the initial giving-bequest gap, which was 8.66 points.

The numbers in the bottom three rows report the *difference* between the baseline gap and the experimental treatment gap. In other words, they report the difference in the giving-bequest gaps as compared with that seen in individuals who had no interventions. (The corresponding numbers for each organization report these results separately for the individual nonprofits tested.)

In brackets is the number of people who responded "yes" to the question regarding whether or not they had a friend or family member who would or would have appreciated their support of the organization (followed by the total number asked the question). This number is also important because the tribute reminder intervention is only relevant for those individuals reporting the presence of a friend or family member who would appreciate (or would have appreciated) their support for the organization. If there are no friends or family members who would themselves appreciate the support of this organization, then there is no basis for a tribute gift.

For example, in the above table, the cancer-related charities were much more likely to have respondents who indicated they had a friend or family member who would appreciate (or would have appreciated) their support for this type of charitable organization. In row three, 216 out of the 486 individuals asked this question responded positively. In contrast, only 58 of 473 responded positively to this question for the wildlife birds organizations. And only 54 out of 466 responded positively to this question for the AIDS organizations. Thus, while the intervention was phenomenally successful for the AIDS organizations in terms of its impact on those who had a deceased friend or family member who would have appreciated their support (corresponding to a massive -16.08 or -24.96 drop in the giving-bequest gap), this applied to a relatively small percentage of the sample.

Although this smaller audience size limits the impact of this type of intervention for some organizations, this factor may not be particularly limiting when marketing to a group that is already supporting the organization. Even if a relatively small percentage of people have a deceased friend or family member who would have appreciated their support of an AIDS organization among the general population, this percentage is likely to be higher among those who are currently giving to such organizations.

The number reported under the "average gap" heading is not the average across all organizations weighting each organization identically. Rather, it is the per person average across all of these organization types. Consequently, the large effects for the AIDS organization are not weighted as heavily as the effects for the cancer organizations, because the AIDS organizations responses represented a smaller proportion of total responses.

> In the group that had first been given the "spendthrift heirs" and "American social norms" marketing messages, the difference was even greater. But, the gap wasn't quite erased.

Interventions	Avg. gap	American Cancer Society	National Cancer Coalition	Dana Farber Cancer Institute	MD Anderson Cancer Center	National Audubon Society	Ducks Unlimited	AIDS Project Los Angeles	San Francisco AIDS Found.
None (Baseline giving-bequest gap)	8.66	9.98	11.98	8.50	9.94	6.91	5.89	7.93	8.11
Δ Memorial alone	-6.20	-5.63 [216/486]	-2.95 [216/486]	-6.05 [216/486]	-6.79 [216/486]	-10.7 [58/473]	-17.1 [58/473]	-16.08 [54/466]	-24.96 [54/466]
Δ Memorial + info 1&2	-7.59	-10.07 [230/488]	-6.55 [230/488]	-11.11 [230/488]	-9.33 [230/488]	-8.18 [55/484]	-0.25 [55/484]	-5.62 [52/478]	-6.57 [52/478]
Δ Honor Living Person + info 1 & 2	-7.84	-6.78 [275/476]	-11.36 [275/476]	-9.08 [275/476]	-9.47 [275/476]	-7.91 [90/473]	-4.11 [90/473]	-4.72 [78/469]	-11.19 [78/469]

The fourth row reports the first results that combine both general marketing messages with a memorial reminder. In this case, we see that the ultimate gap is smaller but has not been completely erased. This group would have first seen the "spendthrift heirs" marketing messages and then the "American social norms" marketing messages prior to responding positively to the memorial question regarding whether or not they had a deceased friend or family member who would have appreciated their support for this type of organization.

Although the gap does not, on average, completely disappear as the result of the combined intervention, it does completely disappear for certain organizations. For example, the American Cancer Society had a baseline giving-bequest gap of 9.98 points. The gap following both "spendthrift heirs" marketing messages and "American social norms" marketing messages and the memorial reminder was reduced by 10.07 points, meaning that the gap completely disappeared. (In fact, in this case, the final stated willingness to leave a bequest gift was slightly higher than the initial stated willingness to make a current gift, among this subset of respondents.)

In contrast, the combined effect for Ducks Unlimited was minimal, coming in at only a 0.25 point reduction in the giving-bequest gap. Note, however that here we are dealing with an exceedingly small sample, totaling only 55 individuals. Consequently, we shouldn't put as much trust in the individual organization numbers. (The average gap column reports the per person average across all organization types, not the per organization average. Thus, it gives less weight to the 55 individuals responding positively to the wild birds organization memorial reminder than to the 230 individuals responding positively to the cancer organization memorial reminder.) Note also that each row represents completely separate groups of individuals. The responses from any one individual could not influence more than one row of results, because each row represents a different combination of interventions and organizations that was given to only one particular group.

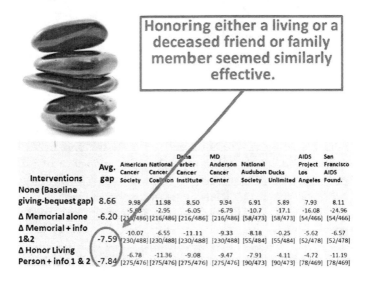

Honoring either a living or a deceased friend or family member seemed similarly effective.

Interventions	Avg. gap	American Cancer Society	National Cancer Coalition	D...a/arber Cancer Institute	MD Anderson Cancer Center	National Audubon Society	Ducks Unlimited	AIDS Project Los Angeles	San Francisco AIDS Found.
None (Baseline giving-bequest gap)	8.66	9.98	11.98	8.50	9.94	6.91	5.89	7.93	8.11
Δ Memorial alone	-6.20	-5.83 [21?/486]	-2.95 [216/486]	-6.05 [216/486]	-6.79 [216/486]	-10.7 [58/473]	-17.1 [58/473]	-16.08 [54/466]	-24.96 [54/466]
Δ Memorial + info 1&2	-7.59	-10.07 [230/488]	-6.55 [230/488]	-11.11 [230/488]	-9.33 [230/488]	-8.18 [55/484]	-0.25 [55/484]	-5.62 [52/478]	-6.57 [52/478]
Δ Honor Living Person + info 1 & 2	-7.84	-6.78 [275/476]	-11.36 [275/476]	-9.08 [275/476]	-9.47 [275/476]	-7.91 [90/473]	-4.11 [90/473]	-4.72 [78/469]	-11.19 [78/469]

In comparing the results from the memorial gift reminder with the living tribute gift reminder in this table, there appears to be relatively little difference in the average results. This is not a definitive test of these two approaches because, of course, these are presented in combination with other interventions and are used on two different and relatively small groups regarding a subsample of only eight nonprofit organizations.

> **For this set of charities, we see the first case where the gap, originally 11.03, completely disappears.**

	Avg. Gap	Prevent Blindness America	Found. Fighting Blindness	The Humane Assn	American Society for Prevention of Cruelty to Animals	Big Brothers / Big Sisters of America	Boys and Girls Clubs of America	YWCA	YMCA	Girl Scouts	Boy Scouts
None (Baseline giving-bequest gap)	11.03	10.82	9.67	11.68	9.59	11.02	12.96	8.21	10.96	14.56	9.05
Δ Honor living person alone	-6.10	-10.37 [66/440]	-7.49 [66/440]	-4.91 [266/451]	-3.50 [266/451]	-3.92 [155/447]	-7.61 [155/447]	-4.08 [155/447]	-7.61 [155/447]	-9.59 [155/447]	-8.28 [155/447]
Δ Honor living person + info 1 & 2	-7.59	-8.92 [67/458]	-9.31 [67/458]	-7.73 [261/469]	-7.71 [261/469]	-3.7 [153/459]	-8.97 [153/459]	-0.24 [153/459]	-7.76 [153/459]	-9.53 [153/459]	-11.21 [153/459]
Δ Memorial + info 1&2	-12.05	-9.89 [43/481]	-8.91 [43/481]	-9.8 [133/492]	-12.97 [133/492]	-14.56 [65/489]	-12.04 [65/489]	-7.29 [65/489]	-15.27 [65/489]	-14.87 [65/489]	-14.43 [65/489]

The above set of results presents a different combination of interventions for a different set of nonprofit organizations. We see first that the suggestion to honor a living person by itself reduced the gap by 6.10 points. This was comparable to the gap reduction of 6.20 points for the memorial reminder alone seen in the previous table for a different set of organizations.

However, in comparing the average change in the giving-bequest intention gap reported in the final two rows, we see our first result that clearly differentiates between the memorial intervention and the intervention of honoring a living person. In this case, the memorial reminder when following the "spendthrift heirs" and "American social norms" interventions produced our first example of the complete elimination of the giving-bequest intention gap among a group of charities.

This is encouraging, but it is important to note that the result is based upon a relatively small number of total observations because none of the charitable organizations in this particular set had a relatively large number of individuals reporting the presence of a deceased friend or family member who would have appreciated their support of the organization. Consequently, we should be more hesitant to have a high level of confidence in this particular result. But, it is both the first result to show complete elimination of the intention gap and the first to show a much stronger effect for memorial bequest gifts than living tribute bequest gifts.

The combination of donor stories and memorial/honoring gifts works every time.

	Avg. Gap	The Amer. Diabet. Assn.	Joslin Diabetes Center	UNICEF	CARE	Guide Dogs for the Blind	Canine Companions for Independence
None (Baseline giving-bequest gap)	10.55	11.70	10.27	11.94	8.83	10.66	10.78
Δ Honor living person + info 3 & 4	-10.59	-12.85 [182/480]	-10.76 [182/480]	-21.53 [74/477]	-13.29 [74/477]	-17.55 [106/471]	-15.87 [106/471]
Δ Memorial + info 3 & 4	-14.60	-13.63 [135/477]	-15.68 [135/477]	-7.70 [66/472]	-7.62 [66/472]	-10.94 [71/467]	-11.63 [71/467]

	Breast Cancer Research Found.	Susan G. Komen Breast Cancer Found.	The Alzheimer's Assn.	The Alzheimer's Found.	World Wildlife Fund	Wildlife Conserv. Society
	11.40	7.83	11.06	10.60	8.26	9.36
	-5.18 [262/487]	-4.78 [262/487]	-10.02 [163/484]	-10.97 [163/484]	-11.18 [202/492]	-14.16 [202/492]
	-12.07 [180/462]	-11.77 [180/462]	-23.69 [152/456]	-24.48 [152/456]	-12.01 [88/463]	-16.97 [88/463]

In the above table, we finally start to see a consistent disappearance of the giving-bequest gap following combined interventions. This is the first table to show the combined impact of the tribute reminders and the "life story" marketing messages. Of course, this result corresponds with the previous findings that the life story interventions were the most powerful general marketing interventions. But it also shows us that these more powerful marketing interventions **can be successfully stacked** with a memorial or tribute reminder to produce tremendous results. When the "life story" interventions were combined with either living tribute or deceased memorial reminders they completely eliminated the giving-bequest intention gap for this subsample of individuals.

Once again, the memorial reminders were more successful than the living tribute reminders, although both completely eliminated the giving-bequest intention gap. The combination of "life story" marketing messages and memorial reminders completely eliminated the giving-bequest intention gap not just overall, but individually for 10 of the 13 organizations tested. This is a powerful result, suggesting just how effective this combination can be for a segment of the population. It is also dramatic to see the magnitude of the result created for the Alzheimer's related organizations. In those cases, the approximately 11 point gap dropped by roughly 24 points. Along with the previous results regarding the AIDS organizations, this suggests that there are certain causes, particularly related to fatal diseases, where such memorial giving reminders can have an unusually large impact.

Conclusion: In this experimental setting, it is possible to eliminate the gap between charitable giving intention and bequest giving intention in certain cases

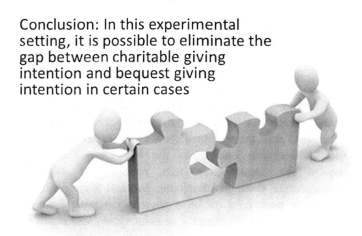

Taken together, these results are quite encouraging. In this experimental setting, it was possible to completely eliminate the gap between charitable giving intentions and bequest giving intentions, at least for those individuals who indicated that they had either a living or deceased friend or family member who would have appreciated their support for the organization. Of course, this is only an experimental setting and even after changing intentions, it is still necessary to convert those intentions into actual actions. But, this experimental result is still tremendously exciting. It suggests that the core problem of a giving-bequest intention can not only be influenced, but can be completely eliminated for certain groups. The ability to stack certain types of interventions suggests the importance of multiple simultaneous messaging on this topic.

As a technical aside, several factors suggest that these experimental results are showing something other than simple social acceptability bias. To begin with, we are examining *the gap* between different kinds of socially acceptable behavior. If an individual respondent had a tendency to overstate their pro-social intentions, this generalized tendency would not necessarily influence our results, because we are comparing only the difference in stated intentions for two different types of pro-social activities.

Another contrary argument would be that we were seeing merely an effect of the intervention exclusively because of the intervention's ability to communicate the socially desirable nature of the behavior. This would require the assumption that support of nonprofit organizations through charitable bequest giving was not previously perceived to be a socially desirable behavior. Even if one were to accept that assumption and claim that the interventions worked exclusively through the ability to communicate the socially desirable nature of the behavior, this would still reflect positively on the intervention as an effective tool to influence intentions. Further, seeing the cumulative impact of multiple interventions, especially the within-person changes from the memorial/tribute interventions which followed marketing interventions, suggests that something other than the respondents' desire to answer in accordance with the investigator's intentions is at work here. This is because the investigator's intentions would be clearly indicated by the first set of marketing interventions. The subsequent impact of memorial reminders could not be explained as the result simply of respondents desiring to answer in accordance with the investigator's intentions, which were fully revealed prior to the comparison set of bequest questions. All of these factors combine to suggest that there is true underlying validity to the results demonstrated in this chapter, even given the reality that these are results from an experimental setting using survey methodology.

The most powerful interventions were:
- **Bequest giving to honor a friend or family member** [NOT for current giving]

- **Stories about deceased or living donors making a lasting impact**

Both fit with related neuroimaging findings

The "take home" message resulting from all of these experimental results is that the two most powerful types of interventions were (1) bequest giving to honor a deceased or living friend or family member, and (2) stories about deceased or living bequest donors making a lasting impact. In addition, these interventions, in combination, were consistently powerful enough to completely eliminate the giving-bequest intention gap. It is also worth noting that both of these interventions also corresponded with the previously discussed neuroimaging findings regarding how people engage in bequest decision-making.

9 PRACTICAL APPLICATIONS
PART I: MANAGING AVOIDANCE

Part IV: Practical Applications to Fundraising

To this point, we have looked at theories and results from a variety of different disciplines and approaches. Ultimately, however, the goal is to be able to make practical applications to fundraising. For the fundraiser who understands the theories and the results, the most powerful applications will typically be the ones that he or she develops himself or herself for his or her particular organization and donor base. However, there are some general principles which should apply to a wide variety of organizations. We will examine some of those general concepts and potential applications here. These applications are suggested by the theories, experiments, and results discussed previously, although not all of them have been verified with experimental lab test or field tests.

Experimental results show that death reminders activate

1st stage defense

2nd stage defense

We begin with the basic concept taken from experimental psychology (terror management theory) which we summarize by describing the two stages of defenses to death reminders. The first-stage defense is avoidance of the death reminders (or the personal implications of the death reminders). The second-stage defense is pursuit of autobiographical heroism (the most extreme version of which is symbolic immortality) based upon support of one's community and community values.

Brain imaging results confirm visualized autobiographical process for bequest decision-making

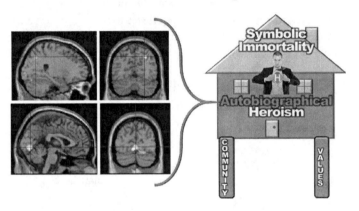

This framework from experimental psychology results in the field of "terror management theory," was consistent with brain imaging results implicating visualized autobiographical processes for bequest decision-making. The alleged pursuit of autobiographical heroism could fit with neuroimaging results that are also consistent with autobiographical processing. In this case, psychological theory, experimental psychology results, and neuroimaging results, are all consistent with the proposed second-stage defense in the context of bequest decision-making.

Using this framework, we can better evaluate communication strategies

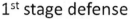

1st stage defense

2nd stage defense

Finding evidence to support the existence of this particular psychological framework for bequest decision-making may be of intellectual significance for researchers, but it won't impact of the daily work of fundraisers until we can use it in a practical way. It is possible. This framework, and the previous results, can be used to better evaluate our communication strategies on the topic of bequest giving. In other words, instead of just thinking, "How would I react to this marketing message?" we can think specifically about how each marketing message or approach would interact with the first-stage and second-stage defenses. These defenses will be relevant whenever we are attempting to communicate on a topic involving mortality salience such as estate planning and bequest giving.

Steps in the bequest decision-making process

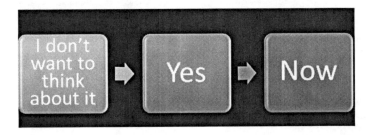

As we begin to apply these theoretical and experimental results, I think it is useful to keep in mind the sequential process for bequest decision-making. Unlike other areas of decision-making, bequest decision-making doesn't start from a reference point of "yes" or "no" or even "I don't know." Instead, bequest decision-making starts from a reference point of "I don't want to think about it." This is the practical consequence of the first-stage avoidance defense whenever we are dealing with issues that create mortality salience.

Ideally we want to be able to move people from the typical beginning framework of "I don't want to think about it," to a new response of "yes." However, this response of, "yes," is not the end of the story. In bequest giving, because of the tremendous impact of procrastination (i.e., avoidance), an additional challenge remains in converting that answer of "yes," into an answer of "now." In other words, for encouraging charitable bequest gifts, the enemy is not usually "no,". The enemy is "later."

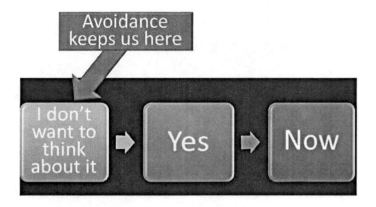

In the first step of the bequest decision-making process, we must recognize that the tendency to respond to mortality salience inducing activities by engaging in conscious or subconscious avoidance works to keep prospects at this first stage of "I don't want to think about it."

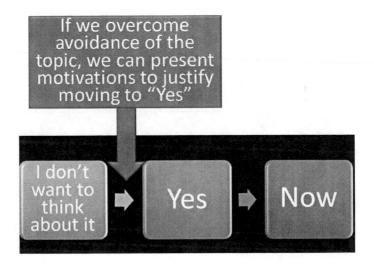

It is only after we can overcome the avoidance of the topic that we can then present motivations to justify moving a person to "yes." In other words, we will never be able to convince someone, or to even open a conversation to convince someone, to move to "yes," unless we somehow are able to successfully overcome the inherent avoidance defense to these topics.

Because overcoming this avoidance defense is central to reaching the vast majority of our supporting donors, we need to first think about how we can overcome the barrier of "I don't want to think about it." We need strategies that answer the fundamental question, "How do you reach an audience with a message that the audience, psychologically, wants to avoid receiving?"

Avoid the Avoiders

- **Only work with those who, due to circumstances (age, health, family death), are ready to charitably plan now**
- **"Low hanging fruit"**
- **Small audience relative to total supporters**

One approach to dealing with the avoidance defense is to simply ignore it. We ignore it by working exclusively with those individuals who have, as the result of outside occurrences, overcome their initial avoidance reaction to the topic. There are a wide range of external circumstances that can cause people to abandon the avoidance defense (i.e., where the avoidance defense is no longer psychologically protective). This can be caused by advancing age, declining health, or the death of a close friend or family member. It could be caused by plans for extensive travel or other activities that people perceive as including a substantial risk of mortality.

Indeed, research on the timing of changes to charitable bequest plans finds that the addition or deletion of charitable plans is often predicated by changes in the perceived risk of mortality or changes in family structure. (see James, R.N. III (2009) Health, wealth, and charitable estate planning: A longitudinal examination of testamentary charitable giving plans. *Nonprofit and Voluntary Sector Quarterly*, 38(6), 1026-1043.) These results suggest that people engage in estate planning through a process that might be described as "punctuated equilibrium." In other words, estate planning is not something that people think about regularly, but only when some outside occurrence creates a shock related to mortality salience or family structure. Because mortality salience is aversive, and therefore estate planning is aversive, we intentionally avoid thinking about it on a regular basis, but instead ignore the topic until one of these outside shocks requires us to deal with the topic.

As a result of one of these outside shocks, simple avoidance is no longer a useful strategy to defend against mortality salience. These are the points of "punctuation" in which most estate planning occurs. Correspondingly, one approach is to focus on those individuals who are at a point of "punctuation" in which they will be most receptive to information related to estate planning. When you reach people during these critical "punctuation" points, avoidance is not a substantial barrier. Often at these critical points individuals are ready to act, and ready to act now. This is an ideal group to work with and clearly should be prioritized given their desire to act and act now. To the extent that we are able to learn of a life event, especially one related to mortality salience, such as diagnosis with cancer, heart disease, or stroke, or the death of a spouse, these "punctuation" points will typically correspond with an increased willingness to learn about estate planning options and complete plans. This is the "low hanging fruit" in estate planning and, as such, these individuals should be prioritized.

However, there are disadvantages to working exclusively with this audience. To begin with, the proportion of supporters who are at one of these "punctuation" points at any given time will be relatively small. Thus, the share of our audience that a message will impact may also be very small. This is consistently reflected in the response rates of mailings that offer free estate planning information, which often hover around 1%

or less. The challenge here is that although the vast majority of people do go through punctuation points when they are open to engaging in estate planning, those points are rare, and sometimes brief.

If we were able to identify when supporters were going through such "punctuation" points, then we could simply wait until such events occurred and enter the picture at precisely the right time to influence a decision. However, this is not the type of information that we typically have for a large group of supporters. We are simply not able to be sufficiently involved with each supporter's life, in such a way that would allow us to identify when these "punctuation" points occur.

This leaves us with the options of either (1) constantly communicating aversive messages that will be inapplicable to 99% of our audience, or (2) somehow learning how to overcome the avoidance barriers of the 99% so that we can convey information that will be helpful and influential during the inevitable "punctuation" points when estate planning decisions are made. Clearly, it seems more efficient when attempting to communicate to a large audience to learn how to manage or, ultimately, to overcome the natural avoidance defense to such topics.

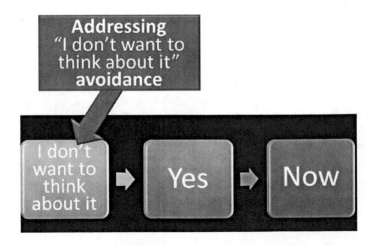

So let's examine the question, "How do we go about addressing the 'I don't want to think about it' avoidance response?"

For many, bequest decision making is emotionally aversive

It is a significant and important first step in the process to recognize that the typical response to estate planning information is going to be avoidance. Simply put, if we understand that, for most people, bequest decision-making is emotionally aversive, it will help us to properly create marketing combinations that will more effectively deal with the problem. As we have already seen, this emotional aversiveness is both a conscious and a subconscious process.

It is not helpful to ignore the problem. (This can be a common mistake, because people designing the messages don't necessarily find them to be aversive. First, people in the field are acclimated to the topics, and second, the messages relate to *someone else's* death.) It is better to simply accept the unfortunate reality that this aversive reaction is not going to go away, it is deep-seated, and for approximately 99% of our audience, it makes the core message uncomfortable. This does not mean that we should despair in being able to effectively communicate this message, or that such communication is a lost cause for the 99% who are not currently in a "punctuation" point in their life. Instead, it simply means we need to recognize this challenge when we are creating our marketing messages.

What you see

What the subconscious sees

To begin with, the terminology that professionals have come to be comfortable with through repeated exposure is not necessarily the best language to use in a marketing context. When we talk about estate planning, we may be contemplating a range of legal, taxation, and document drafting topics. However, when addressing the topic of estate planning for non-practitioner audiences we are, at least at the subconscious level, presenting on the topic of the person's upcoming death. The topic for the planner is not aversive in part because it isn't focused on the planner's own personal mortality, but rather the mortality of audience members. Additionally, practitioners tend to focus on charitable, legal, and tax implications of such planning. But, for the individual client or donor these issues are secondary to the reality that the plan is for his or her upcoming death. So if our core topic is fundamentally, even subconsciously, aversive to our intended audience, what can we do?

Mixed Packaging
The topic is subconsciously aversive, so combine (or mask) with more attractive topics to sidestep the initial avoidance response

An initial approach to presenting an aversive topic, such as estate planning, is to mix it with other less aversive topics, so as to sidestep the initial avoidance response. This fits with the phrase from the Mary Poppins song that "a spoonful of sugar helps the medicine go down." If we don't recognize that the topic is consciously and/or subconsciously aversive, then we will simply present the aversive topic in a process that blatantly broadcasts the unpleasant nature of the information we have to present. Everything we know about this topic suggests that the "frontal assault" approach will fail to reach all but the 1% or so who are no longer using the first-stage avoidance response.

If we want better responses, then we need to think of

creative and clever ways to engage in "mixed packaging." These are ways in which we can communicate the necessary information so that the audience has the knowledge and tools that they will need during those future "punctuation" points in which these decisions will be made. But we may have to "slip in" this information as a minor part of some other communication activity in order to avoid the natural avoidance response that would otherwise block the communication as a whole.

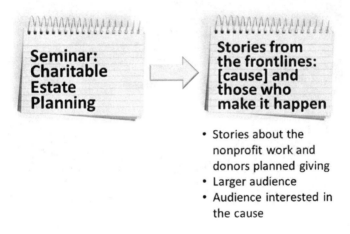

So how might this be done? First, we can look at this issue in the simple context of presenting an informational seminar. It is not uncommon to communicate about charitable estate planning by presenting informational seminars. If we simply label the seminar as one on estate planning or charitable estate planning, then we will likely reach only a very small segment of our desired audience. The aversive response to mortality salience will cause the great majority of our potential audience to avoid the seminar.

So how can we reach a larger audience? We reach a

larger audience by engaging in "mixed packaging" where we combine the charitable estate planning information with more positive, interesting, and attractive topics. So instead of having a seminar on "Charitable estate planning," we may have a seminar on "Stories from the front lines: Cancer research and those who make it happen." The seminar would include stories about the work of the nonprofit (such as the cutting edge research conducted by cancer researchers supported by the nonprofit), but we would also include stories about donors who make the research possible. Within these stories about donors who make the research possible, we would include examples of donors who have supported the research through sophisticated planned giving or deceased donors who have supported the research through simple bequest giving.

Through these stories, we then communicate the information and techniques that will be helpful to the audience members when they engage in estate planning decision-making in the future. It is especially helpful whenever we can encapsulate this information in the form of a story. The human brain is specifically designed to capture, retain, and recall information in the form of stories. Further, the neuroimaging results suggest that the decision-making processes may be more "visualized autobiography" than, for example, number comparison or financial calculation related. Because many bequest donors will not involve the charity in their planning processes, it is critical that information is conveyed in such a way that it will be "sticky", and consequently available during the future time when such decisions are made.

Seminar: Estate Planning and Christian Stewardship → **Seminar: Christians and the Government**

- Include estate planning components along with "hot button" religious liberties topics
- "The state has written your will for you and they cut out your church. Are you OK with that?"
- Larger audience

Here is another example of the importance of seminar titling taken from my own experience as a practitioner. For a number of years, I worked as the director of planned giving for a religious college that, among other things, engaged in training preachers, ministers, and missionaries. Thus, it was common for us to make presentations in local churches often on a Sunday afternoon or Sunday evening. Copying what had been done in the past I initially began making these presentations as "estate planning" seminars or perhaps "estate planning and Christian stewardship" seminars. I learned very quickly that this kind of presentation drew a remarkably sparse audience.

This result makes sense in the context of the current theory, because I was presenting an aversive topic by means of a "frontal assault." My results changed dramatically when I changed the seminar title and content to be less aversive and more generically interesting. I could give a seminar on "Christians and the law," or "Christians and the government" and get a much larger audience. Of course, this did alter the contents of the seminar substantially. We discussed a wide variety of religious liberties topics that were of great interest related to religious freedoms and current political controversies, but one-third of the seminar related to those government or legal issues relevant to estate planning. I was able to obtain dramatically larger audiences and simultaneously learned how to communicate the core pieces of critical estate planning knowledge in a more condensed, and probably more memorable, fashion.

This was only the first key to the dramatic increase in charitable planning that took place as a result of the seminar change. The second change dealt with the barrier (which we will discuss later) of moving people from "yes," to "now." This was addressed by creating an immediate deadline. People who were at the seminar had the opportunity to immediately sign up for an initial consultation timeslot for the following day and could receive a free simple will. However, the offer was only available if they signed up immediately. Thus, we created a deadline and a reason to shift from "yes," to "now." The one-shot deadline was critical in triggering action. Giving people more options and more choices led to much less action, whereas giving them a single "now or never" option produced exponentially greater compliance. But, of course, that very effective "now or never" immediate opportunity would not have had a substantial audience if the topic had not been presented in the context of attractive mixed packaging.

Seminar: Charitable Estate Planning → **Seminar: New Ways to Save More Taxes When You Give**

- Encompasses a wide range of planned giving topics including estate planning
- Income qualifies audience based on who will be interested in the topic

Another example of repackaging a seminar on charitable estate planning is to present a seminar on "New ways to save more taxes when you give." Although tax benefits are rarely the primary motivator for donors, tax benefits are not an aversive topic. As a result, this is a subject that is of general interest among those who are financial supporters to an organization, and it does not highlight the death-related nature of some parts of the information. As before, the topic advertised is more broad. The contents of the seminar would also necessarily be more broad. The new seminar would encompass a wide range of current and planned giving topics. But, critically, it would include the important information related to estate planning.

The (potentially aversive) estate planning information is included in a way that, while being consistent with the topic, is not broadcasted by the title. This particular topic heading also has the advantage of speaking to a qualified audience, meaning an audience who both has interest in charitable giving and are at such an income/deduction level that additional tax deductions are of significant interest. Thus, we can prequalify an audience in a positive way but still retain a substantial group to whom we can present the (inherently aversive) estate planning information as part of a larger group of topics.

Manage Avoidance
A series of bequest related messages in a general interest donor publication

Ignore Avoidance
A donor-wide mailing labeled as "estate planning"

The concept of mixed packaging can be used in a variety of marketing channels. For example, if we recognize that the topics are aversive, we can add them in as minor components in publications that are of general interest to our target population. This, of course, means that the messages will need to effectively communicate key concepts in relatively few words. The goal is to include these sidebar brief statements without making the publication piece as a whole aversive to the larger audience.

If instead we ignore the natural avoidance response and use a donor-wide mailing prominently labeled as "estate planning," we are more likely to have a complete rejection of the information being presented. Although we may send out a massive amount of mailings, if we don't recognize the inherently aversive nature of the topic and mix it with more attractive pieces, we are likely to fail in the effort to ultimately communicate the necessary information to our audience.

Use a broad survey to learn and teach

Which of the following areas do you consider to be the most important for this organization?
□ Student scholarships   □ Scientific research
□ Classroom teaching   □ Community outreach
□ Other: _____

Were you aware that, for those over age 55, donating the future inheritance rights to your home or farmland creates an immediate income tax deduction of 70% or more?
□ Yes   □ No   □ Uncertain
□ I would like more information about this

Another example of a piece that allows communication of planning information in the context of a larger communication piece with a separate, but related purpose, is the use of donor surveys. We begin with a survey for the purpose of learning the opinions and values of supporting donors. This survey must have its own separate (and organizationally-respected) purpose aside from communicating gift planning information. But, within the context of a broad survey intended to collect information about donor priorities, values, and interests, critical information-communicating questions can be included within the survey.

For example, if you are in a low interest rate environment with AFRs near 1% you might include a question asking, "Were you aware that, for those over age 55, donating the future inheritance rights to your home or farmland creates an immediate income tax deduction of 70% or more?" Here we are referring to the donation of a remainder interest deed in a home or farmland which is a relatively lesser known planned giving technique. By reading and responding to the question, the donor has received and understood the core planned giving concept that might motivate future action. But, the communication is done in the context of a broad survey on multiple topics, so as to not create an aversive communication vehicle. If instead we were to create a survey on "Your knowledge of charitable estate planning," we would expect to see a very low participation rate, because we would have packaged the survey entirely as one about an inherently aversive topic (i.e., your death).

There are, of course, a wide variety of other potential applications of the "mixed packaging" strategy. How this might apply to your organization will differ from other organizations. Nevertheless, the basic concept is always the same. We engage in mixed packaging or masking of the aversive topic in order to reach a larger audience that we can then educate about bequest giving opportunities. Once we have the audience, we can — in brief and innocuous ways — communicate critical nuggets of information to that larger audience. Ultimately, the goal is to be able to move a larger number of people away from the base state of "I don't want to think about it" to the desired state of "yes, that's a good idea."

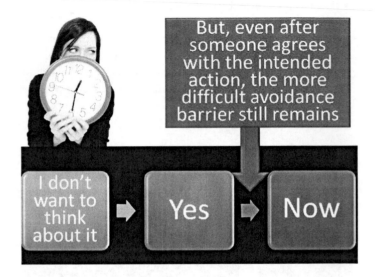

Moving people from "I don't want to think about it" to "yes, that's a good idea" is an absolutely critical goal. But it is not the end goal. To achieve cognitive assent to an idea is useful, but by itself it will not produce revenue for the organization. In other realms of marketing, there is not a substantial barrier between reaching "yes," and generating action. However, in the context of estate planning, the barrier between "yes" and actual action is the most difficult barrier. Before we congratulate ourselves on reaching a larger audience and convincing that larger audience that they should engage in the action, we need to recognize that this is not the hardest step in the process. The hardest step in the process is moving from "yes" to "now."

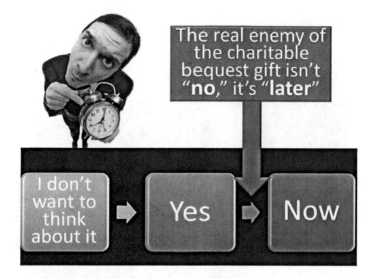

Another way to put this is to recognize that the real enemy of the charitable bequest gift isn't "no," it is "later." A variety of surveys of charitable donors, or even the general population, show widespread agreement with a willingness to consider including a charity in a future estate plan. However, this relatively widespread agreement with the concept of, and even intention to engage in, charitable estate planning is not matched by actual post-death transfers. This difference can be on the order of a tenfold magnitude. For example, where maybe 5% or 6% of decedents actually generate charitable bequest transfers at death, it would not be shocking to see 50% to 60% agreement with a general willingness to consider including a charitable recipient in an estate plan to be completed at some point in the future.

This demonstrates the magnitude of this most difficult barrier of moving people from *agreement with the concept* of leaving a charitable bequest gift to *actual behavior* that generates a charitable transfer at death. How can we attempt to address this most difficult barrier to actual post-mortem charitable transfers at death? Let's examine some of the considerations.

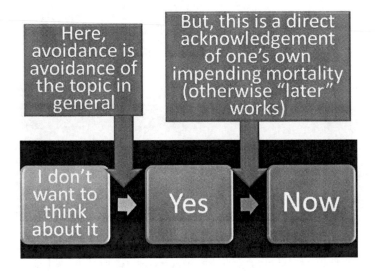

One of the reasons that this second step is so much more difficult is that it is more closely tied to personal mortality, in particular to impending personal mortality. It ramps up the aversive nature of the message. When we wish to communicate about estate planning concepts in general, we have to deal with the general aversiveness that relates to a death-related topic. But when we try to get people to complete final documents, we are dealing with the aversiveness of directly acknowledging one's own mortality. Beyond this, we are often dealing with a necessary recognition of one's own IMPENDING mortality. Why? Because *if* the risk of mortality was *not* impending, then it would be appropriate to respond by simply answering, "yes, but later."

Why now?

If I am not going to die tomorrow, why not deal with this unpleasantness later?

The critical issue is simply this: if I am not going to die tomorrow, why not postpone this unpleasant activity? Logically, we have to be able to answer the question of "Why now?" If moving from "yes" to "now" is an inherently highly aversive process, we have to justify why the action should not be completed later. The enemy of the bequest gift is not "no." The enemy of the bequest gift is "later." And "later" is always a logical response if I am not going to die tomorrow. So how can we deal with this seemingly appropriate and logical objection?

A common initial response is to point out the obvious statistical reality that impending death is always a possibility. We might be tempted to respond to the issue by saying, "But, you might get hit by a truck tomorrow."

As natural as that response may seem, everything we

know about the avoidance defense suggests that this is a bad argument. It is not that the argument is statistically invalid. Rather, it's that the natural avoidance response to mortality salience will cause a rejection of the suggestion, regardless of its statistical validity.

People simply don't want to admit, psychologically, the potential for immediate mortality. Such an admission is psychologically painful and people will not be inclined to truly accept such arguments. Just as we saw with experimental psychology results where participants altered their statistical analysis when the predictions related to their own risk of mortality, if we make the same argument here, we are working against the natural biases that we know exist in humans. We make the type of argument that is specifically designed to be ineffective when we approach the issue by emphasizing the potential for imminent mortality.

This
delay
bias is
(almost)
always
confirmed

"See, I told you I
didn't need to
plan yesterday"

Further, this bias towards delay – driven by the highly aversive nature of the action and the lack of necessity for the action in the absence of impending mortality – is repeatedly confirmed by that the fact that the client did not die yesterday. Their lack of death means that they did not need to have previously engaged in planning, and postponement was completely appropriate.

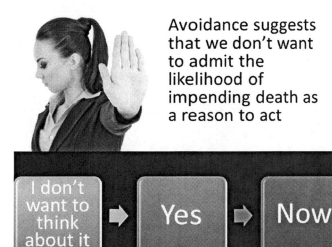

Avoidance suggests that we don't want to admit the likelihood of impending death as a reason to act

People operate with a clear bias that is consistently confirmed in experiment and practice. We want to move people from "yes" to "now," but the argument about the risk of immediate death will be largely ineffective. So what do we do?

So create another reason...

If the argument against delay based upon the risk of immediate mortality is not going to be successful, then we need to create another reason for action. We need to have a response to the question, "If I am not going to die tomorrow, why not deal with this later?" How might we do this?

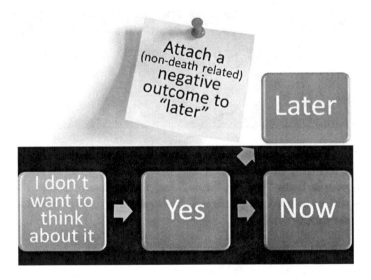

In order to deal with the tendency to choose later rather than now, we must be able to attach a negative outcome to the choice of acting later. In particular, we would like to attach a negative outcome to the choice of acting later that is not related to the risk of immediate mortality (because we know that such arguments will naturally be rejected at both the conscious and subconscious levels). We can do this by either attaching a negative outcome to choosing later, or by attaching a temporary positive outcome to choosing "now," (which consequently makes the "later" option relatively negative). What are some examples of this?

As discussed previously, one method that I used successfully over a number of years was to offer a free simple will service for anyone who signed up for an appointment immediately following the seminar. While the offer of a free simple will was, perhaps, in and of itself attractive, this was not the critical component of the offer. The critical component was that the opportunity was available only for immediate action. The service could not be accessed later. If instead the participants had been offered a free simple will consultation available any time at their convenience, the response rate would have been much lower. The open-ended offer would not address the question of, "Why not do it later?" If there is no difference in opportunities between now and later, prospects will tend to choose later. (This returns us to the situation where the only advantage of engaging in the unpleasant activity now is in the event of unexpected imminent death, which is an occurrence that people naturally discount.)

In this sense, the offer attaches a relatively negative outcome to the "later" choice. The negative outcome to the "later" choice is that will preparation will be more expensive when choosing "later" rather than "now." This negative result of the "later" choice is easy to accept, because it does not rely upon recognizing the immediate risk of personal mortality.

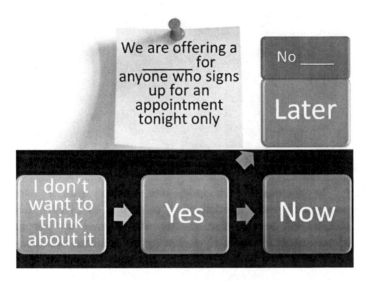

The critical key to the effectiveness of the previous strategy was not just that it provided a free service related to estate planning, but that it attached a negative consequence to postponing the estate planning. In a similar way, if we were to offer any type of benefit or service for an individual who agreed to act immediately, we might expect positive results. The idea is to intentionally attach a (non-death related) positive outcome to acting now that will not apply to acting later. This provides a motivation to act that does not require a conscious acceptance of the probability of immediate death.

The benefit need not be attached to signing documents, but simply attached to signing up for an appointment and arriving. Of course, signing up for an appointment is not the end goal. The goal is to generate a post-death transfer, which requires signing a legally enforceable document. But, signing up for an appointment begins that process. More importantly, that first appointment can then be tied to an additional appointment (ideally a signature appointment) so that postponement means missing an agreed upon appointment. In this way the process takes on an inertial force, with social costs for breaking the process.

Of course, if we attach a benefit to signing up for an appointment and that appointment then does not result in a subsequent meeting to either sign or otherwise advance towards signature of a plan, then the problem of persistent postponement ("later") will arise again.

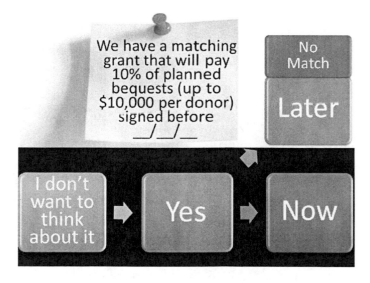

One attractive way to consider attaching a relatively negative outcome to postponement is to create a matching grant. For example, a charity might advertise a matching grant that will pay 10% of planned bequests, perhaps limited to $10,000 per donor, signed before a campaign deadline date. Obtaining the funds for such a matching grant proposal would not necessarily be difficult when working with a donor who was in the process of making a gift of this magnitude anyway. Showing the donor the potential multiplicative impact of the gift when established as a matching fund to encourage charitable bequest planning in others could be compelling.

Certainly, a signed revocable document could be changed. There is no guarantee of the ultimate impact of the matching fund. But, if the donor was going to give the large sum of money in either case, then the risk that some of the signed bequests would ultimately be changed should not be a problem. (Any additional bequest gifts are preferable to no additional bequest gifts.) An explanation of this type of matching approach can be found in Michael Rosen's book *Donor-Centered Planned Gift Marketing*.

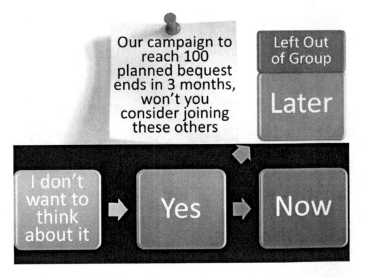

How else might we attach a positive result to acting now, and a negative result to acting later? The idea of creating deadlines and attaching them to fundraising goals is central to most fundraising campaigns. We can use this same methodology to create goals related to reported gift planning. For example, one organization I worked with created a two-year campaign to reach 100 planned legacies.

This campaign created a deadline and a goal. It was followed by a celebration dinner honoring those who had participated in the campaign. This presented an opportunity to communicate about the success of the campaign through regular updates in general interest donor publications. Additionally, it created a reason to bring up the topic when visiting with donors for other purposes.

By creating a goal and a deadline, this approach attached a relatively negative consequence to planning later. Planning later meant that the person would not help the organization to reach the goal and would be left out of the group that made the goal happen. Subtly, it may have also suggested that postponing beyond such a long window of opportunity was tantamount to a refusal rather than simply a delay.

Such a campaign-related opportunity could be especially influential for those in leadership such as board members. Such leaders often recognize, or can be made to understand, the importance of their role in setting a high standard to encourage others in supporting the organization. They can participate as a way of influencing others. Further, the argument does not rely upon an acceptance of the risk of immediate personal mortality. Although people may resist recognizing the risk of their own immediate mortality, they are quite rational in recognizing the probabilities for mortality in others, such as those donors whom they can influence through exemplary behavior.

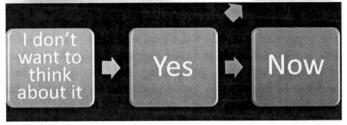

In addition to these self-created deadlines and opportunities, there are similar deadlines and opportunities that may be created from the environment. For example, the section 7520 rates change monthly and these rates influence the deduction available for certain types of planned gifts. For those prospects considering such planned gifts, the change in the 7520 rate might be used to encourage immediate execution of a gift. Typically, the donor can use the 7520 rate from the current or the previous two months. This creates a natural "expiration date" for attractive rates. For example, if the rates were 2.5% for the current month, 2.4% for the previous month, and 2.3% for the month before that, this creates a situation where the low rate of 2.3% will be available only for a few more days.

This expiring rate can be used to create a natural deadline for completing a planned gift by pointing out the penalty for delay (i.e., the lower tax deduction). For example, if a donor is interested in leaving a bequest gift of an interest in a home or farmland and wishes to leave that bequest gift in such a way that generates an immediate tax deduction, the donor would be considering signing a remainder interest deed. The deduction available for signing that deed is greater to the extent that the 7520 rate is lower. Consequently, the sequence of 7520 rates can be presented as a disappearing opportunity with an *immediate* deadline as a way of motivating the donors to *immediate* action.

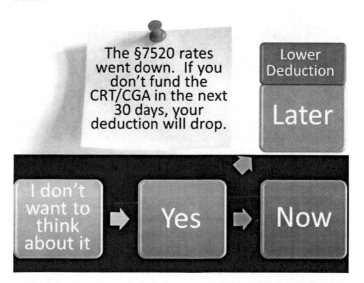

Conversely, other planned gifts result in a higher deduction when the 7520 rates are higher. (For example, a Charitable Remainder Trust is presumed to earn interest at the 7520 rate for the lifetime of the trust. A higher presumed earning rate for a trust paying a fixed annuity, would leave a larger amount for the charity at the expiration of the trust.) In either case, the goal is to emphasize the importance of acting now because of the negative outcome of acting later (such as a lower deduction). Ultimately, the goal is simply to motivate immediate action.

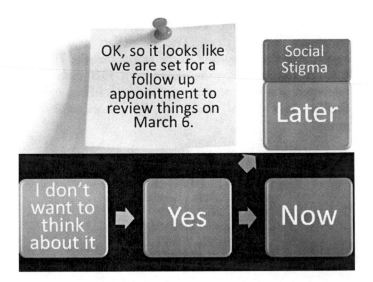

Attaching a negative result to postponement may be as simple as setting an appointment. If a prospect agrees to meet with a fundraiser to review completed documents at a specific date, then failing to complete those documents means that he or she will either have to cancel the appointment or keep the appointment and admit that the intention to complete the documents was not achieved. Either of these options has a limited amount of social stigma attached to it. Consequently, simply establishing an appointment date with expected completion of a goal attaches a negative outcome to delaying planning beyond the appointment date.

Essentially, this creates a deadline. To the extent that a fundraiser can be successful in establishing additional appointment dates during each meeting, he or she can attach deadlines (with minor social consequences) for each step in the estate planning process that ultimately leads to a signed enforceable document.

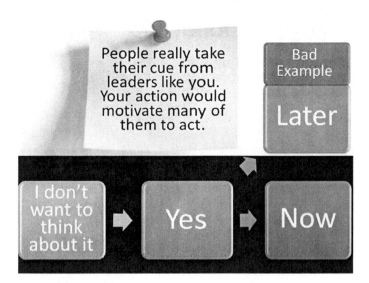

If we attach a campaign deadline to making a bequest commitment, this can provide a special opportunity for those in organizational leadership (such as members of the Board of Directors) to commit to engaging in bequest planning, simply as a way of influencing others to engage in the activity. Conversely, if the leader chooses not to participate in the campaign, it may be viewed as setting a bad example, thus attaching a negative consequence to the decision to delay engaging in the planning. Again, what is important is that postponing planning beyond a specific date creates negative social stigma, which serves as a negative outcome unrelated to one's personal risk of immediate mortality.

Pledge and follow-up

Consider promoting and
recognizing non-binding
simple check box "pledges"

*I commit to complete
an estate plan with a
gift to (organization)
within 6 months*
☐ *Yes*
☐ *No*
☐ *Already
Completed*

Such social stigma can be enhanced through the use of simple non-binding pledges to act. Pledges can be successful for a couple of reasons. First, the pledges create a scenario where a person must physically act in order to report an intention to postpone the planning. Recall the results discussed earlier showing the massive behavioral differences in organ donation depending upon whether the system was structured in an "opt-in" or "opt-out" framework. We take advantage of this understanding by using the pledge checkbox to attach a positive action to saying no (or even "later") in response to a request to complete a charitable estate plan.

Of course, unlike the organ donation context, simply checking a box has no legal consequence. But the non-binding pledge is the critical first step in the pledge and follow-up process. Once the prospect has made a commitment to complete the charitable bequest plan prior to a deadline (in this case six months later), postponing planning beyond that deadline is attached with the negative social consequences of failing to fulfill a personal commitment. The attention paid to this negative

240

consequence can be enhanced by subsequent follow-up.

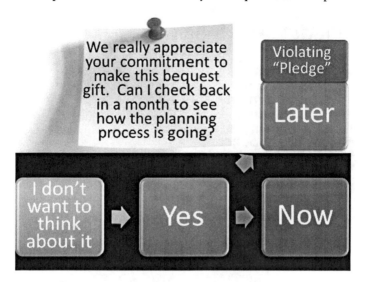

For example, following such a commitment, the prospective donor could be contacted to inquire about the status of his or her planning. In a very pleasant way, the fundraiser could

(1) Thank the prospective bequest donor for his or her commitment.
(2) Emphasize the importance of that commitment, both for the organization and potentially for influencing the action of other prospective donors
(3) Simultaneously check on the progress of the planning process, thus attaching a mildly negative social consequence of having to admit a lack of success on the intended action.

Such a contact would be difficult, or perhaps even inappropriate, in the normal setting. But, because of the previous pledge of planned activity, the reminder contact becomes appropriate and acceptable. Thus, rather than creating a commitment to immediately complete a process, the pledge creates a commitment that is initially relatively agreeable because of the distant completion date.

Pledge and follow-up

"To show a strong leadership commitment in this planned giving push, we want to announce 100% board participation by the fall banquet. Can we count you in?"

I commit to complete an estate plan with a gift to (organization) within 6 months
☐ *Yes*
☐ *No*
☐ *Already Completed*

Such commitments can be enhanced when they are presented as a component of organizational leadership, especially when they are presented as a way to create an example that would be followed by others. Thus, the reason for requesting the commitment could be to demonstrate the importance of the behavior to other supporters. As mentioned before, this is helpful because it is a reason to engage in planning that has nothing to do with personal risk of immediate mortality. Thus we might combine a commitment card with an ask such as "to show a strong leadership commitment in this planned giving push we want to announce 100% board participation by the fall banquet. Can we count you in?" This creates a deadline, a motivation, and social benefits attached to the commitment.

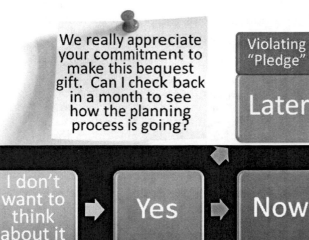

Of course, the simple checkbox commitment is not the end of the story, but it creates the opportunity to engage in regular follow-up to ensure that the initial commitment is completed.

As mentioned before, the power of defaults in death related decision-making is particularly strong.

> ### Board Member / Group Pledge Form
>
> To influence other supporters of this organization, we are looking for leaders who will demonstrate the importance of planned giving. In preparation for the July announcement of the planned giving campaign kick off please let us know.
>
> ☐ **I have already included [org] in my estate plans**
> ☐ **I will commit to completing an estate plan with a gift to [org] before July 5th**
> ☐ **I do not have [org] in my estate plans and I cannot commit to doing so**

The use of a pledge form which has options for "yes," "no," and "already completed" means that inaction is not an appropriate response. Supporters, especially those in leadership, often do not want to intentionally state that they have no interest in supporting the organization through a bequest plan. Such a negative statement is undesirable and may conflict with the way that they perceive themselves. Even though engaging in estate planning may be aversive, if the aversive act is sufficiently far into the future then the it is much more attractive. In other words, the checkbox option of agreeing to complete a charitable estate plan by some date substantially in the future *feels* like the desirable "later" response, but the difference is that this "later" response is not generically later (leading to eternal delays), but rather is a specific "later" response with a deadline.

It is the commitment to a deadline that then allows the fundraiser to engage in a series of follow-up communications. The follow-up contacts become more powerful, because people have a natural desire to act consistently with their stated commitments.

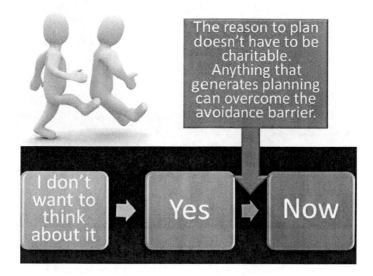

Although the barrier from of moving from "yes" to "now" is substantial, it does not have to be overcome by strictly charitable motivations. In fact, it is probably most often the case that this barrier is overcome as the result of factors completely unrelated to charitable intent. Anything that generates planning activity will, by itself, overcome the avoidance barrier. If we have a prospect with an underlying interest in leaving a bequest gift, we can use any type of planning motivation to get them to engage in the planning process. What matters is not whether the motivation relates to the charity, but simply whether or not it causes the planning activity.

For example, a person might desire to update his or her estate plan because a family member is not named in the estate plan, due to the age of the document. Although it may be of no particular legal consequence, the person might believe that the youngest child who was not named in the document might have bad feelings if he or she learned of this. Postponing updating the will thus has a potential negative consequence associated with it that is unrelated to the risk of death. (Here the risk is that the unnamed child might learn the details and resent that the older siblings were named and that he or she was not.)

Similarly, a client might risk negative feelings if the children found out that someone else was named as executor. This discovery could occur even prior to death, and so doesn't necessarily have to be attached to the risk of immediate mortality. Again here, people are psychologically more willing to accept the risk that the document might be inadvertently read by another person than that they might experience near-term death.

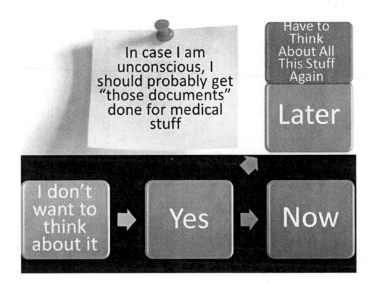

This motivation to plan for noncharitable purposes could also be generated by the need to complete other death-related planning documents for medical purposes. For example, if a person preparing for surgery is encouraged to complete a living will or medical power of attorney, he or she might be convinced to engage in updating all estate planning documents simply as a way to get through all of the unpleasant death-related planning at once. In this way, the aversive nature of the documents is used to justify their completion all at one time. In other words, if we are going to have to complete some death-related documents (which is unpleasant), we might as well complete them all, so that we don't have to think about it again for a long time.

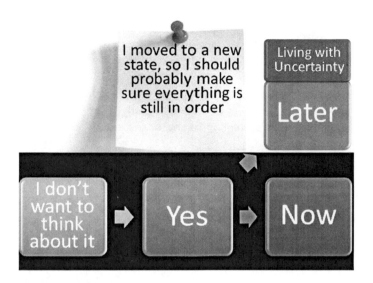

Other factors can motivate engaging in estate planning, such as simply moving to a new state. In that case, if I postpone planning, then I have to live with the uncertainty of not knowing if my previous documents would be treated the same in my new state.

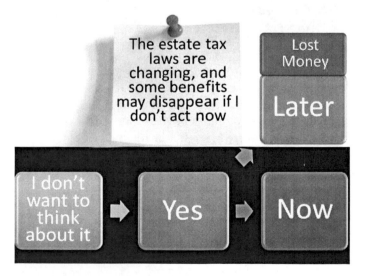

Similarly, as the tax laws change, there may be scenarios where some estate tax benefits could disappear if no action was taken. This appeared to be the case at the end of 2012 when the estate tax exemption was scheduled to drop substantially, thus encouraging gifting that would take advantage of the higher exemption amount prior to its expiration.

It's also useful to consider that not all planned giving options work against the natural tendency to avoid recognition of the potential for immediate personal mortality. Those options which provide a lifetime income to the donor, either through a charitable gift annuity or a charitable remainder trust, may be particularly attractive to the extent that prospects perceive that they are going to live a long time. In that sense, these options are much more attractive psychologically because they are not necessarily viewed as death planning documents.

10 PRACTICAL APPLICATIONS PART II: BUILDING AUTOBIOGRAPHICAL RELEVANCE & SYMBOLIC IMMORTALITY

To this point we have focused on dealing with the first-stage defense of avoidance. Avoidance initially can prevent prospects from leaving the "I don't want to think about it" stage.

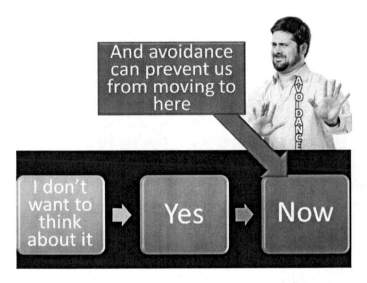

Additionally, avoidance can prevent prospects from moving from the "yes" stage to the "now" stage. Instead, avoidance suggests that the preferable response is not "now" but rather "later."

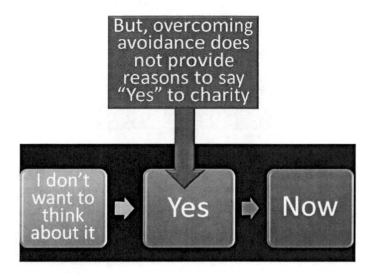

The strategies we've examined so far have looked at how to overcome these two avoidance barriers. Avoidance can keep prospects from leaving the "I don't want to think about it" stage and prevent prospects from moving from the "yes" stage to the "now" stage. But, overcoming the avoidance barrier does not provide any motivation to say "yes" to charity. Overcoming avoidance can get people to think about the topic, and it can get them to act upon their desires. But, overcoming avoidance does nothing to encourage a person to have charitable bequest desires.

Overcoming avoidance can clearly can lead to estate planning. But it does not necessarily encourage charitable planning, except to the extent that prospects have pre-existing charitable bequest desires. Can we do more than that? Can marketing go beyond simply encouraging planning and actually encourage charitable planning? Can we present charitable options that are motivating to prospects beyond their generic interest in the charity itself?

Some might suggest that the answer is "no." Perhaps the only goal in charitable bequest marketing is to motivate those with pre-existing charitable intent to complete plans. This is certainly a reasonable idea. If we could wave a magic wand that compelled all of the donors to a particular organization to complete their estate plans, that by itself would dramatically increase the ultimate bequest dollars transferred to the charity. It is clearly an important goal (and it could be the only goal). But even more can be achieved if we move beyond simply getting everybody planned and instead consider how to increase charitable desires, perhaps even creating new charitable products that are inherently attractive to significant segments of donors.

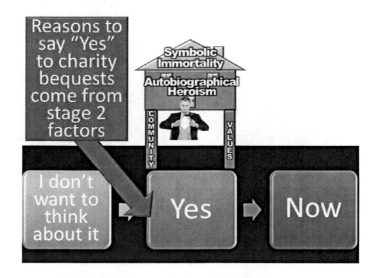

So where do we find these motivations to say "yes" to charity in a bequest context? These motivations come, not from the first-stage avoidance defense, but from the second-stage factors. Avoidance is something to be managed, something to be overcome. But avoidance is not motivational. What motivates the bequest gift (in the context of death-related decisions) are these second-stage factors of symbolic immortality and autobiographical heroism based upon one's community and community values.

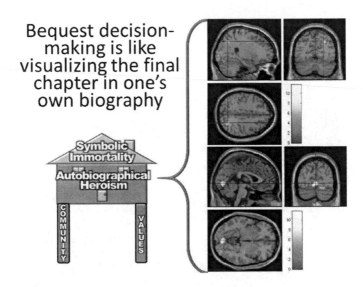

What do we know about these motivational factors? We know from the neuroimaging results that bequest decision-making could be analogous to visualizing the final chapter of one's own biography.

This result suggests that a key question in considering whether to include a particular charity will relate to the prospect's own autobiography. In other words the prospect asks, "Is this cause or this charity an important part of my life story?" If the cause or the charity is not an important part of the prospect's life story then it doesn't belong in the final chapter of his or her autobiography.

How can we emphasize autobiographical connections?

Given the importance of connections with prospects' life stories in motivating a charitable bequest, what can we do to emphasize these connections? Obviously, different options will be available to different kinds of charities, and the best will depend upon the creativity of the individual organization's fundraisers. However, let's look at a few examples that might help to generate some creative ideas.

Start with

"So tell me about your connection to (organization)."

When speaking with donors, we want to begin with statements or questions that encourage them to think about their life story connections with the organization or the cause.

DON'T start with

"I've got some great ways to get you some huge tax deductions."

Although we may ultimately get into complex planning techniques including a wide range of tax benefits, this is unlikely to be the best starting point for a conversation. The bequest decision-making processes appear to differentially engage autobiographical processes *not* mathematical processes. This means that the decision to benefit a charity will relate to the prospect's own visualized autobiography. The technicalities of the plan come only after the decision has been made to benefit the charity in an estate plan. Thus, we start by emphasizing autobiographical connections, "So tell me about your connection to the organization," and not "I've got some great ways to get you some huge tax deductions." This doesn't mean that taxation-related topics will not ultimately be of interest, but it means that these are not typically going to be the factors that determine the desire to leave a charitable bequest gift.

Recognizing and rewarding donor longevity (not just annual levels) emphasizes the long-term autobiographical connections

Our 10 Year Anniversary together. 29 gifts totaling $1240. Thank you!

Understanding donor motivations related to autobiography also suggests how we might want to recognize our donors. For current giving purposes, it is a common and appropriate practice to recognize donors for their annual giving level. However, a different emphasis may be appropriate to encourage bequest giving.

Recognizing donor longevity (rather than the previous year total amount) emphasizes the long-term autobiographical connections of the donor with the organization. A longevity recognition could be for the number of years, in total, in which a donor has made a gift of any level to the organization. The years not need not necessarily even be consecutive, because the point is to emphasize the "life story" connection with the donor. Recognizing donors for having given for 5 years, 10 years, 15 years, or more, presents clear evidence of the autobiographical connections between the donor and the charity. The recognition helps to solidify that the donor's identity and life story are defined, in part, by his or her long-term commitment to the organization. In this context, it doesn't matter if those gifts were $10 gifts or $10,000 gifts. What matters is consistency in support over a long period of time, which makes the charity part of the donor's life story.

Alumni magazines that dwell on the good old days

Alumni magazines for universities that dwell on "the good old days" can be particularly useful and effective at emphasizing the autobiographical or "life story" connections between donors and the organization. While these may not provide an immediate appeal for writing a current gift check, they build the life story connections that are essential when decisions are made regarding bequest giving. The presence of nostalgia may be a critical motivating factor in one's attachment to the charity, especially given what we know about the visualized autobiographical processes involved in charitable bequest decision-making.

Donor functions that encourage socializing with long time friends associated with organization

Similarly, donor functions that encourage socializing with friends who are also associated with the organization emphasize the autobiographical connections between the donor and the organization. To the extent that one's social circle (community) is integrated with the charity, then bequest gifts that support that community and social circle will be particularly attractive. As discussed previously, in the presence of death reminders (as in estate planning), interest in supporting one's community and community values increases. To the extent that a donor participates in a community which has the shared values of supporting a particular charitable cause, the likelihood for charitable bequest gifts should increase.

Heroic Biographical Modeling:
Lionize deceased bequest donor autobiographies

Recognizing that donors engage in this decision-making process using visualized autobiography suggests the potential power of other donor autobiographies in motivating action. Of course, we don't have to speculate on this, as the previously discussed experimental results strongly confirmed the particular power of donor biographical stories in influencing intentions to leave a charitable bequest.

Offering donors the opportunity to leave gifts with permanence can increase the motivation to leave bequest gifts.

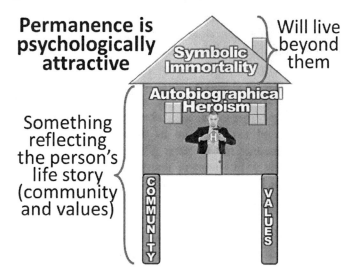

Permanence is psychologically attractive, given an

underlying idealized goal of symbolic immortality. The idea of symbolic immortality is simply that something reflecting the person's life story, their community and their values, will live beyond them. To the extent that we can create giving opportunities which themselves have permanence, it increases the donor's ability to achieve some form of symbolic immortality.

Recall that, in the previously discussed experimental results, the impact of sharing data regarding rapid expenditure of inheritances by non-charitable heirs was particularly influential on the bequest decisions of those over age 50. People don't like the idea that when they die, this world will not be any different than it would have been if they had never lived. This thought is psychologically unpleasant. As a defense against this psychologically unpleasant prospect, it is natural to desire that something reflecting one's life story, one's community, and one's values will live beyond one's personal death.

When a charity provides the opportunity to make a bequest gift that will continue to have an impact, not just immediately after the death of the donor, but for many years to come, the charity provides an opportunity that is psychologically very attractive (especially in a context where a donor is contemplating his or her own inevitable personal mortality). This was also supported by the previous experimental results showing that respondents who expressed a difference in their preference desired more permanence for bequest gifts than current gifts by approximately a two-to-one margin. There is something special about bequest gifts that creates a relatively greater desire to make a lasting impact.

	Normal Group Average Gift	Death Reminder Group Avg. Gift
Immediate Focused Charity	$257.77	$80.97
Permanent Focused Charity	$100.00	$235.71

A poverty relief charity was described as an organization that focused on either "meeting the immediate needs of people" (Immediate Focused) or "creating lasting improvements that would benefit people in the future" (Permanent Focused)

*54 participants giving share of $1,000 award (Wade-Benzoni, et al., 2012)

The above slide displays results from a recently published study by Dr. Kimberly Wade-Benzoni at Duke University and colleagues. In this experiment, participants were all entered into a lottery to win $1,000. Participants were told that they could pre-commit to share part of the $1,000 with a charity, if they happened to win the prize. The charity was the same for all participants, but for half of the participants the charity was described as "meeting the immediate needs of people," and for the other half it was described as "creating lasting improvements that would benefit people in the future." (The idea here was to emphasize either immediate impact or permanent impact.) In the first two groups (which read an unrelated newspaper article before making these choices), those receiving the immediate impact description committed, on average, to give $257.77. However, those reading the permanent impact description committed only $100.00 on average.

A second set of groups completed the same choice. However, before they completed the choice, they read a death-reminder article about a recent tragic airplane accident that had resulted in death. The impact of permanence switched in this death-reminded group. Specifically, the death-reminded group receiving the immediate impact description of the charity pledged only $80.97 on average. However, the death-reminded group receiving the permanent impact description of the charity pledged $235.71.

The results suggests that preference for permanent gifts dramatically increases after exposure to a death reminder. The researchers concluded, "death priming leads individuals to be concerned with having a lasting impact on other people in the future"(Wade-Benzoni, et al., 2012, p. 704). This is a dramatic experimental demonstration that in a decision setting with high mortality salience – like estate planning – permanent gifts will be particularly attractive.

Lasting gifts (endowments, named buildings, scholarship funds, etc.) to stable organizations may be particularly compelling

As a result of this underlying desire for permanence (potentially related to the pursuit of symbolic immortality) certain types of gifts and certain types of organizations may be particularly attractive. Lasting gifts such as endowments, named buildings, or scholarship funds made to organizations that are perceived to be stable provides an excellent opportunity for achieving some measure of symbolic immortality. If a donor makes a gift that results in a named building at Harvard University, he or she will have a high level of confidence that his or her name will continue to be on that building when children, grandchildren, great-grandchildren and so forth would happen to visit the campus. The donor reasonably believes this because of a high confidence in the stability of the organization.

However, donors may achieve this same level of permanence, or in reality an even greater level of permanence, by giving money to a named endowment or permanent fund. A donor can feel confident that this named fund will continue to accomplish important goals aligned with the donor's community and values long after the donor has died. This is an ideal type of gift to address the psychological difficulties associated with focused contemplation of personal impending mortality.

Organizational age helps
(perceived stability and donor age)

% of gift income from bequests and founding date of UK cancer charities among Top 100 UK fundraisers
(Pharoah, 2010)

Cancer Research UK	42.6%	(1902)
Macmillan Cancer Support	37.9%	(1911)
Marie Curie Cancer	31.0%	(1948)
CLIC Sargent Cancer Care for Children	18.6%	(1968)
Breast Cancer Care	2.1%	(1972)
Breakthrough Breast Cancer	1.0%	(1991)
Walk the Walk Worldwide	0.0%	(1998)

Data from Pharoah (2010)

Related to this notion of organizational stability is that bequest donations may be relatively more common among organizations that are older. The relationship between bequest gifts and organizational age could come from perceived stability as well as from the age profile of the donors supporting the organization. Older organizations may be advantaged because they are seen as being more likely to exist for a long time in the future. Older organizations may also be advantaged because of the long-term relationships with older donors.

Although there are no statistics in the United States from multiple types of nonprofit organizations to compare the dollars raised from current gifts to the dollars raised from bequest gifts, that information is available for charities within the United Kingdom. The previous table shows the percentage of gift income from bequests for each United Kingdom cancer charity listed among the top 100 United Kingdom fundraising organizations. In looking at the percentage of gift income from bequest gifts, we see a clear relationship between the age of the organization and the share of gift income that comes from bequest gifts.

If your organization is new, consider marketing permanent funds managed and administered by, e.g., a large financial institution to borrow feelings of strength and stability

The previous result should not be interpreted as suggesting that younger organizations should not be concerned with bequest gifts. Every revenue stream is essential to accomplishing the mission. The bequest income coming to a younger organization does not become less important simply because an older organization receives a larger percentage from its bequest gifts. But it could suggest that newer organizations might want to consider emulating the characteristics of older organizations in terms of perceived stability and, where possible, the age profile of donors. One possibility to consider for a new organization is to market permanent funds that are managed and administered by a large community foundation or financial institution in order to borrow feelings of strength and stability from those older and larger organizations. Even if a nonprofit is relatively new, it can market the establishment of endowment funds managed by a large community foundation. In this way, even if the organization doesn't project a sense of tradition, stability and longevity, it can still borrow that sense of stability and longevity from another organization.

Even if the newer charity closed, the fund itself could still continue supporting similar goals.

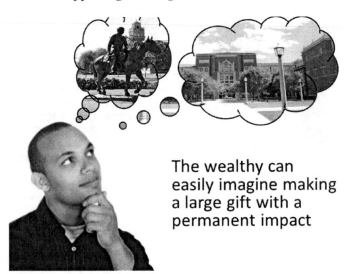

The wealthy can easily imagine making a large gift with a permanent impact

When considering the importance of permanence in bequest giving, it is useful to consider that for the wealthy, imagining making a large gift with a permanent impact is relatively easy and natural. It is easy to think of permanent gifts available to someone willing to transfer millions of dollars. From buildings to endowments to private family foundations, the options are varied and often obvious.

Consider developing permanent giving opportunities for mid-level bequest donors

- Scholarships, lectureships, annual performances, perpetual child sponsorship, perpetual rescued pet sponsorship, etc.
- Limit to legacy donors to emphasize specialness and avoid pulling from current giving

However, one potentially critical role for the fundraiser is in developing permanent giving opportunities for the mid-level bequest donor. It is easy for a donor to think about permanent giving opportunities if he or she can pay for an entire building or an entire new wing added to a hospital. But for the mid-level donor without the ability to transfer massive sums of money, such permanent opportunities will depend more on the ability of the nonprofit organization itself to create and market them.

A permanent giving opportunity may be something as simple as agreeing to accept and manage permanent endowment funds. The charity need not market these as endowment funds. They could be labeled based upon the purpose for which the funds are going to be used. For example, various charities could market a perpetual child sponsorship fund, or a perpetual rescued animal sponsorship fund, or a permanent lectureship fund, or a permanent scholarship fund, and so forth. The purpose for a fund will relate to the individual charity's cause.

But, these are the kinds of permanent giving opportunities that are often particularly attractive to donors who are making these decisions in a context of high mortality salience. In other words, these are the kinds of opportunities that give donors the chance to achieve some slice of symbolic immortality that fits with their chosen community and community values.

In some organizations, marketing permanent endowment-type funds may appear at odds with the desperate need for immediate dollars. One potential resolution of this conflict that particularly encourages charitable bequest giving is to create permanent fund opportunities that are available only for bequest donations. Thus, an organization can market and attract mid-level permanent funds without fearing that current giving dollars are going to be diverted away from much-needed immediate expenditures. Limiting such opportunities to bequest gifts emphasizes the specialness of bequest giving. More importantly, it provides donors with the type of giving opportunities that are particularly motivating for bequest giving.

Or mid-level memorial donors

Symbolic Immortality

Permanence

Life Story

Dear [Memorial Donor],

Please allow me to take this moment to extend our gratitude for your generous contribution in memory of John P. Smith. We are honored that you would choose to recognize the life of John through this gift to [charity]. [Charity] has been committed to [cause] for over X years, working in diverse fields such as...

In accordance with our memorial gift policy, we have established the **John P. Smith Memorial Fund**. This fund will provide resources sufficient to [ongoing project example] at an estimated annual expenditure of $500 annually. At most recent account the total gifts to this fund, including your contribution, have reached $1,612. Thus, we anticipate this fund will actively support the work of [charity] until its expiration in August of 2016. However, should the fund reach the minimum threshold of $10,000, it will become perpetually self-sustaining and will be renamed as the **John P. Smith Permanent Memorial Endowment**.

As a contributor to this fund, we will keep you updated as to the financial status of the fund and the impact that these gifts are making. However, if you do not wish to be updated on the status of this fund in the future, please check the box on the enclosed postage-paid card and we will respect your wishes.

Once again let me express my gratitude for your thoughtful gift to the **John P. Smith Memorial Fund**.

Sincerely,

Executive Director
[Charity]

Although at the time of this writing, this has not yet

been experimentally tested, it might be possible to extend the permanence opportunity to memorial donations. The above letter describes how such a presentation might be made to memorial donors. Theoretically, such an approach could have a powerful psychological impact, because it presents the opportunity to have a permanent remembrance of one's deceased friend or family member. Here money given in memory automatically goes into a memorial fund and upon reaching a minimum threshold level becomes a permanent memorial endowment. If the minimum threshold is not met, then the fund pays out and expires at a preset rate.

The motivation to convert to a permanent fund may be particularly high given the natural desire for applying symbolic immortality to recently deceased friends or family members. This is an example of how underlying theoretical knowledge might be used to develop innovative new strategies in a variety of circumstances. (I hope in the future to be able to field test the efficacy of this strategy.)

Create a memorial wall of heroes listing all bequest donors.

(Consider adding some connection to their life stories – graduation date, restricted fund designation, "lover of cats", city of residence, etc.)

Make donors think, "I want to be on that [permanent] wall"

Symbolic Immortality

Permanence

Life Story (community and values)

As another example of applying our understanding of

bequest related psychological processes, a charity might consider creating a memorial wall of heroes, listing all deceased bequest donors. This, of course, would be especially helpful in charities where donors are likely to visit the location of the memorial wall. It could also be quite helpful to add information related to the decedents' life stories and how theirs lives connected with the particular charity.

This could be easier, or more challenging, depending upon the charity type. For example, a school graduation date and degrees earned would be a natural way to connect one's life story with the university. Other information might relate to the specific restricted fund to which the bequest was directed. City of residence, surviving relatives, or essentially any information that created a permanent statement of symbolic immortality linking to the decedent's autobiography could have a positive effect. The goal is for prospective donors to be able to visualize the wall when they are in the midst of estate planning. The non-profit wants donors to think, "I want to be on that wall." Although not yet experimentally tested, this is another example of a plausible idea which springs from an understanding of the psychological and neurological processes involved in bequest decision-making.

The permanent opportunity must still align with one's community and values.

"Why would I want my name on a permanent endowment fund to rescue neighborhood cats? I don't even like cats."

There are a variety of different ways to develop opportunities that emphasize permanence. However, the desire for symbolic immortality, as the highest expression of autobiographical heroism, must always be based upon the foundation of the prospect's chosen community and community values. It will have no effect to develop the most attractive permanent giving opportunity if the prospect's values do not align with the organization or the cause.

Using the model to rethink use of media

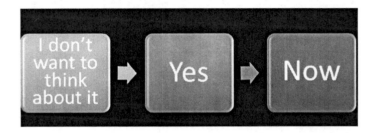

In addition to using the model to develop new types of giving opportunities, this framework of understanding can also help to reframe how we use different marketing channels.

Charitable products and media can...

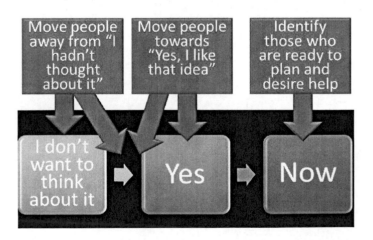

If we understand the bequest decision-making process as having three stages ("I don't want to think about it," "yes," and "now"), we can apply this understanding to the role of media marketing. The development of attractive charitable products related to bequest giving and communication about charitable bequest giving through media can accomplish a lot. First, media channels can move people away from "I don't want to think about it" and towards, "yes, I like that idea." Further, media can identify those who are ready to plan and desire immediate assistance in that planning process.

Broadcast media, however, may not be very well suited to move people from having a general intention to make a charitable bequest to actually executing documents. That move generally is motivated either by direct personal involvement of a fundraiser or, more commonly, by some external circumstance, typically related to mortality or change of family structure, that motivates the person to engage in new planning.

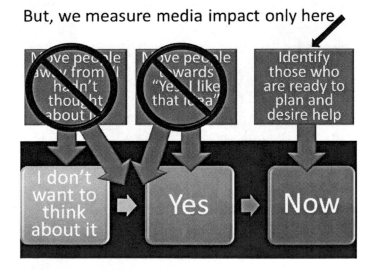

But, we measure media impact only here

Move people away from "I hadn't thought about it"

Move people towards "Yes, I like that idea"

Identify those who are ready to plan and desire help

I don't want to think about it → Yes → Now

Given that media and charitable products have great

potential to move people from "I don't want to think about it" to "yes," it is unfortunate that most measurements of bequest giving marketing tend to emphasize only the identification of those who are immediately ready to plan and desire assistance with that planning. This measures only the very small segment of any group that is in an immediate planning mode at any one time. This focus on such a narrow group in such rare circumstances ignores the most powerful parts of charitable bequest gift marketing. In other words, a response rate of 1% or less to an offer of providing estate planning materials or assistance completely ignores the impact of the marketing messages on the other 99%.

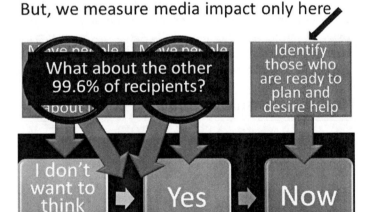

This leads to the obvious question of, "Why are we not measuring the impact on the other 99%+ recipients of charitable bequest marketing materials?"

As most bequests are "unknown" to the organization in advance, this is a critical goal

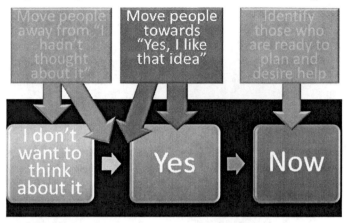

Measuring this shift in intentions is much more important for charitable bequest fund raising than for current giving fundraising. In current giving fundraising, we can measure the success of an appeal letter based upon its ability to generate immediate gifts. (It would even be possible to run a regression analysis to see if a particular letter generated an increased or decreased level of future current gifts within the next several months.) But that type of measurement tradition works against successful measurement in the area of charitable bequest marketing.

Unlike current giving, most charitable planning actions take place without the knowledge of the charity. So we are not going to passively receive the same kind of feedback that we receive when we are marketing for current gifts. Estate planning itself is not a regular part of life, but instead takes place during those punctuation points usually caused by increasing mortality salience or changing family structure. If we can move prospects to have a general intention to make a charitable bequest gift, at some point outside interventions will likely generate the motivation to engage in new planning. (Or, alternatively, a series of

279

personal visits from a fundraiser may also provide such motivation.)

So, measure it

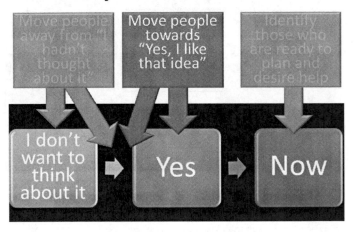

Given the importance of changing people's attitudes about leaving a charitable bequest gift, it makes sense to seriously consider measuring that change in attitude among an organization's supporters.

Include in regular surveys about donor priorities an attitudinal question about bequest giving:

> "If you completed a will in the next 3 months, what is the likelihood that you might leave a bequest gift to (charity): none, I don't know, slight possibility, some possibility, strong possibility, definitely would"

- Simply getting people to answer moves past "I hadn't thought about it"
- Eliciting overt statements of intent can change choice during later planning

How might we go about conducting this measurement? It could be done in the same way that attitudes towards other topics are commonly measured every day. If a charity is willing to conduct regular surveys about donor priorities and preferences regarding the charity, it is then a relatively easy matter to include a single question related to bequest giving intentions. Asking a question as simple as, "If you completed a will in the next three months, what is the likelihood that you might leave a bequest gift to this charity?" allows tracking the indicator across time.

Such measurement does not require mailing a survey to the entire donor base repeatedly. Instead, it could involve mailing to a relatively small, randomly selected subset of donors on a regular basis. For example, if a charity mailed a questionnaire to 10% of their donor base every quarter, then an individual donor would see a survey only every 2 ½ to 3 years. This is not a burdensome amount of communication, either for the charity or for the donors. But, it would create a quarterly measurement of attitudes related to bequest giving. In other words, it would create a measurement of the impact of charitable bequest marketing on the other 99% of donors who are not interested in requesting immediate assistance with estate planning. Naturally, a 10% sample can vary somewhat from quarter to quarter simply because of the particular people who responded to the survey in that quarter. Thus, not every single movement of the number would be important. Nevertheless, such tracking creates a scientifically useful basis for measuring the impact of charitable bequest marketing over time. A person with a research orientation could even consider mailing different pieces to different parts of the sample to see which marketing piece had the greatest effect on expressed attitudes. Such a strategy not only provides an excellent measurement of the impact of bequest marketing on the 99% of nonrespondents who, ultimately, will be critical in generating actual post death charitable transfers, but it is also independently influential in encouraging completed charitable bequests.

Responding to a question related to one's intentions to leave a charitable bequest to the organization accomplishes two important goals. First, it gets people to move past the "I don't want to think about it," stage by intentionally "thinking about it." It does so in a format that is not aversive, because it is simply one single question in the context of a brief survey about other organization-related topics.

Additionally, getting people to make a statement of intent can crystallize that intention in such a way as to increase the propensity for them to actually engage in the behavior. This crystallized intention becomes especially important when outside circumstances necessitate engaging in new estate planning. Thus, simply getting donors to answer the question is, for multiple reasons, an important victory in encouraging charitable bequest giving. This is aside from the fact that regular measurements of donor attitudes creates a concrete, immediate outcome in a field where such meaningful measurements are few and far between.

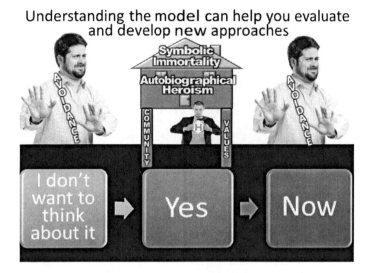

Understanding the model can help you evaluate and develop new approaches

To summarize what we have learned to this point, the above graphic visually represents the underlying model of how bequest decisions are made. We have examined a variety of scenarios in which understanding this model leads to particular proposals for charitable bequest marketing strategies. But, ultimately the most important value of understanding this model of charitable bequest decision-making is that this understanding can be applied to any organization in any situation to create brand-new marketing products and strategies.

The most important practical value of understanding the model will come from your own brain and how you can apply the model to the particular circumstances of your situation for your charity and your particular group of donors. Starting with an underlying model that is verified by neuroscience results, experimental psychology results, experimental charitable bequest giving research results, and psychological theory, provides the solid framework and footing which can lead to truly transformational methods to encourage charitable bequest giving for your organization.

11 USING THE MODEL TO UNDERSTAND YOUR TWO BIGGEST COMPETITORS

Applying the model to understand your two biggest competitors for charitable bequest gifts

At this point we have looked at scientific evidence underlying the model. And we have looked at a variety of different applications of the model and how it can be used to generate successful ideas and methodologies for encouraging charitable bequest giving. Next, we will look at how the model applies to your two biggest competitors. Now, when I refer to your two biggest competitors I am not referring to other public charities who serve your same cause, or who are located in your same city. Those are not your biggest competitors. In many ways, these organizations are in the same boat as your organization. It is quite common for bequest donors, especially female donors, to name a wide variety of charitable recipients. However, 90% of your significant donors will die, leaving no charitable bequest gift. They are not leaving gifts to your competitor charities, because they are not leaving gifts to any charities. The biggest reason for that relates to the number one most important competitor for charitable bequest gifts. And, by this point, you have probably guessed who that number one competitor is. It is the prospective donor's offspring, his or her children and grandchildren.

#1. Children/ Grandchildren

From the perspective of the bequest decision-making

model, children and grandchildren are an ideal expression of symbolic immortality. They reflect the donor's life story and are intimately connected with the donor's community and values. And they will live beyond the donor's life. It is no surprise then that the bulk of all bequest transfers go to children and grandchildren (after there is no surviving spouse).

So how can we use this information? It makes sense and it fits the model, but how is it helpful? Initially, it can be helpful when it helps us to recognize the importance of childlessness as a predictor of engaging in charitable estate planning. When we are able to identify a supporter who is not "burdened" by having these natural competitors, we should recognize that supporter as a potentially high value bequest giving prospect. Let's look at some national numbers that support this supposition.

Among Donors ($500+/year) over age 50 with an Existing Estate Plan

Family Status	% indicating a charitable estate plan
No Offspring	50.0%
Children Only	17.1%
Grandchildren	9.8%

2006 Health and Retirement Study, 10,113 respondent households, weighted to be nationally representative

The above table shows results from a large survey weighted to be nationally representative. Here we are looking only at individuals who make annual donations to charity of $500 a year or more, who are over the age of 50, and who have an existing estate plan. Of course, this group of older donors with estate plans will be, as a whole, much more likely to have a charitable estate plan than the general population. But what is notable from this table is the massive difference between charitable bequest planning among those with no offspring, and those with children or grandchildren. A donor who gives over $500 a year, who is over age 50, with an existing estate plan, who has grandchildren has less than a 10% chance of having included a charitable beneficiary in that plan. However, a similarly-situated person who has no offspring has a 50-50 chance of having a charitable beneficiary in their plan. This single demographic factor is associated with a massive difference in the propensity to engage in charitable bequest planning, and it should be respected as such when prioritizing the prospects for bequest giving communication and solicitation.

Regression: Compare only otherwise identical people

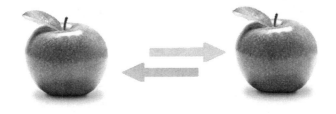

Example: The effect of differences in education among those making the same income, with the same wealth, same family structure, etc.

Next we examine regression results that compare otherwise identical people. By using regression, we are able to make an "apples to apples" comparison between individuals who are otherwise similar. This is especially important for a variety of factors that might influence charitable behavior. For example, we might say that those with a higher education are more likely to make charitable gifts. But that association may be caused by the tendency of higher education to generate higher income, and it may be the income and not the education that is actually causing the increased likelihood of charitable giving. If we want to actually understand the separate influence of education, aside from its association with increased income, then we have to use a regression technique. Regression allows us to compare people of the *same* income who are different in their level of education. In this way we can really begin to uncover how powerful a particular factor is, by itself, in predicting the outcome of interest.

Likelihood of having a charitable plan

(comparing otherwise identical individuals over age 50)

- Graduate degree (v. high school)   +4.2 % points
- Gives $500+ per year to charity   +3.1 % points
- Volunteers regularly   +2.0 % points
- College degree (v. high school)   +1.7 % points
- Has been diagnosed with a stroke   +1.7 % points
- Is ten years older   +1.2 % points
- Has been diagnosed with cancer   +0.8 % points
- Is married (v. unmarried)   +0.7 % points
- Diagnosed with a heart condition   +0.4 % points
- Attends church 1+ times per month   +0.2 % points
- Has $1,000,000 more in assets   +0.1 % points
- Has $100,000 per year more income   not significant
- Is male (v. female)   not significant
- Has only children (v. no offspring)   -2.8 % points
- Has grandchildren (v. no offspring)   -10.5 % points

The above table provides results from a regression measuring the likelihood of having a charitable plan (in this case, the results are generated by a probit model and report the marginal effects of each element assuming all other variables were set to their sample means). This shows the separately identifiable impact of each variable on the likelihood of having a charitable plan, comparing otherwise similar individuals over the age of 50. Keeping in mind that approximately 6% of these individuals will have a charitable estate plan, we can see the relative importance of various factors.

For example, having a graduate degree increases the likelihood of having a charitable plan by 4.2 percentage points. Giving $500 or more per year to charity increases the likelihood of having a charitable plan by 3.1 percentage points. Volunteering regularly increases the likelihood of having a charitable plan by 2.0 percentage points. However, having grandchildren as compared with having no offspring decreases the likelihood of having a charitable plan by 10.5 percentage points.

Find your bequest donor...

A
makes substantial
charitable gifts,
volunteers regularly,
and has
grandchildren

B
doesn't give to charity,
doesn't volunteer,
and has no children

For a simple illustration of what these results mean, consider the following comparison. Suppose there are two older adults and we want to predict which one is more likely to leave a charitable bequest at death. Person "A" makes substantial charitable gifts, volunteers regularly, and has grandchildren. Person "B" does not give to charity, does not volunteer, and has no children. We might naturally think that the person who regularly volunteers and makes substantial gifts to charity would clearly be more likely to be a bequest donor. In that case we would be naturally wrong. Statistically speaking, the person who has no children or grandchildren is more likely to leave a charitable bequest, even though he or she doesn't volunteer or make current charitable gifts. This illustration shows the importance of appropriately targeting those who have no offspring.

From an Australian study by Christopher Baker including 1729 wills:

"Australian will-makers without surviving children are ten times more likely to make a charitable gift from their estate."

Results from Australia suggests that this phenomenon is not limited to the United States. My colleague (and sometime co-author) Christopher Baker examined 1729 wills in Australia and concluded that "Australian will makers without surviving children are 10 times more likely to make a charitable gift from their estate." The point here is not that we should be surprised that those without children are more likely to leave a charitable bequest. The point is that the magnitude of that factor in determining who leaves a charitable bequest is massive and should not be ignored. If we were to give a precise weight to that factor in an analysis of a set of donor records, how much weight should we give it? The next table attempts to answer that question.

Estate giving and annual giving for 6,342 deceased panel survey members

Offspring	Last Annual Volunteer Hours	Average Annual Giving	Average Estate Giving	Estate Gift Multiple
No Children	32.6 (6.6)	$3,576	$44,849	12.6
Children Only	25.4 (7.1)	$1,316	$6,147	4.7
Grandchildren	23.2 (2.1)	$1,497	$4,320	2.9
Total	24.3 (1.8)	$1,691	$8,582	5.1

The above table shows the estate giving and annual giving for a little over 6,000 people who were in a longitudinal survey and died during the course of that survey. The results show that, on average, those with no children left an estate gift of approximately 12.6 times their average annual giving. The group with grandchildren left an estate gift of approximately 2.9 times their average annual giving. Thus, a quick and easy methodology for comparing the relative value of donors in terms of bequest gifts would be to apply these estate gift multiples to their average level of giving. (For a more sophisticated approach to modeling this valuation see my forthcoming publication on national charitable estate giving statistics.)

Factors that triggered dropping the charitable plan

1. Becoming a grandparent	0.7226* (0.2997)
2. Becoming a parent	0.6111† (0.3200)
3. Stopping current charitable giving	0.1198* (0.0934)
4. A drop in self-rated health	0.0768† (0.0461)

Some factors that didn't seem to matter:

Change in income

Change in assets

Change in marital status

*Fixed effects analysis including 1,306 people who reported a charitable plan and later reported no charitable plan. Coefficients show relative magnitude of factors.

This next set of results is different because it looks at the timing of dropping a charitable plan. Although the individual numbers shown here are not directly interpretable as percentages, they show the relative magnitude of each factor. In this analysis, only four factors were statistically significant in predicting that a charitable plan would be dropped. The number one most important factor was becoming a grandparent. The number two factor was becoming a parent. Much less significantly was ceasing all current charitable giving.

These results once again emphasize the idea that the biggest competitor for charitable bequests are offspring, both children and grandchildren. As a side note, changes in income, assets, or marital status were not significant in predicting dropping a charitable component out of an estate plan in this particular analysis.

Family bequest decision involve more emotion (mid/posterior cingulate cortex; insula) and memory recall (hippocampus) than charitable bequest decisions.

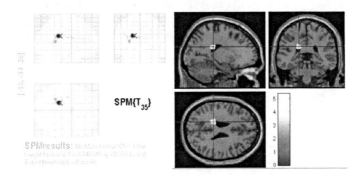

SPM{T₃₅}

These previous statistical results also fit with the neuroimaging findings that family bequest decision making involves more emotion and memory recall than charitable bequest decisions.

How can a charitable bequest compete with this level of emotion and memories?

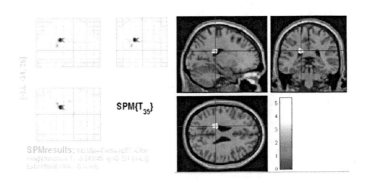

SPM{T₃₅}

So given that these type of family bequest decisions are so much more common and naturally involve so much more emotion and memory than charitable bequest decisions, how can charities compete?

How can a charitable bequest compete with this level of emotion and memories?

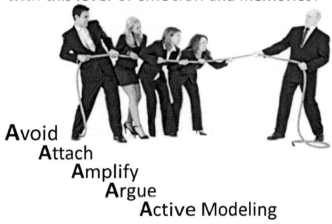

Avoid
   Attach
      Amplify
         Argue
            Active Modeling

This is not a lost cause. Charities can compete with bequest gifts to family members. As we attempt to compete with this most significant natural set of competitors, we can think about strategies categorized into the 5 A's. Next, we will examine each of the strategies of avoid, attach, amplify, argue, and active modeling.

Avoid

Avoid the strongest competition (i.e., focus on those without children/grandchildren)

The first strategy in competing with other bequest recipients is to simply avoid those who have children or grandchildren. In other words, whenever possible spend time cultivating older prospects who are childless.

Attach

The emotion and memory associated with a deceased "loved one" may be attached to a cause representing the person

A second strategy is to attach the emotion and memory associated with a deceased "loved one" to the nonprofit cause representing that person. We've already seen the experimental results that show just how powerful this strategy can be in changing attitudes towards bequest giving.

For the bequest donor with a deceased "loved one," the charity may provide the only realistic method to give "to" the deceased "loved one". Thus, the charity does not need to independently generate emotion and memory in the donor. Instead, the charity simply attaches its cause to the pre-existing memory and emotion associated with the deceased "loved one." Surprisingly, the experimental results showed that attaching a charity to a living friend or family member through a tribute bequest was almost as effective as attaching the charity to a deceased friend or family member. Both sets of results suggest that it is possible to attach the emotion and memory associated with another person to a charitable cause and through that attachment to increase the desire to benefit that charitable cause through a bequest gift.

Attach

"Loved one" can include furry family members. Among top 100 UK fundraising organizations, 7 of the highest 15 bequest income percentages were held by domesticated animal charities (Pharaoh, 2010).

Although the experimental results described previously measured the impact of memorial or honoring gifts for a friend or family member, it is probably more appropriate to use the generic term of "loved one," given the popularity of animal charities as recipients of bequest gifts. When examining the 100 largest fundraising nonprofits in the United Kingdom, domesticated animal charities represented seven of the highest 15 nonprofits in terms of the percentage of income raised through bequests. Conceptually, some of this charitable bequest activity may relate to the desire to create a lasting memory (autobiographical heroism) for a family pet. Although the "loved one" is different, the concept of attaching the cause to the pre-existing emotion and memory engendered by a deceased or living "loved one" is essentially the same.

Attach

Model by sharing stories of those who immortalized deceased loved ones with a permanent bequest gift

We can encourage this form of attachment by sharing models. In other words, we can share stories of those who have immortalized deceased loved ones with a permanent bequest gift. This creates both a reminder for those who were aware of the possibility and education for those who were not aware of the possibility of leaving such a bequest gift. Such modeling fits with the visualized autobiographical mechanisms common to bequest decision-making.

Amplify

Build the charity's emotional and memory connections with the donors

Of course, if we are not borrowing the emotion and memory attached to another individual, we must rely upon the emotional and memory connections with the charity itself. This, of course, is a general development goal that is shared with all parts of the organizational fundraising team. It is one of many examples where success in one area of development improves the chances for success in other areas of development. The methodologies used to amplify the charity's emotional and memory connections with the donors are as varied as the organizations that use them. This simply points out that success in these areas may ultimately also express itself in success in the area of charitable bequest donations.

Argue

Leaving 100% to family is
Not required.

If you received an inheritance where 10% of the estate had gone to the person's favorite charity, would you feel unhappy about their decision?

Potentially harmful.

Leave "enough money so that they would feel they could do anything, but not so much that they could do nothing." – Warren Buffet

Temporary.

On average, 1/2 of inheritance is spent immediately and more than 1/3 of heirs quickly spend it all (Zagorsky, 2012) v. permanence and significance of charitable opportunities.

The next approach is to make logical, rational arguments. Here we use rational arguments to show the limits to the benefit of leaving funds to children or grandchildren and the acceptability of leaving some funds to charitable organizations. These arguments could take a variety of different forms, some of which were tested in the previous experimental results.

For example, emphasizing the temporary nature of gifts given to heirs due to the propensity of a substantial share of heirs to quickly spend their inheritance was tested and found to have a modestly positive effect on intentions to leave a charitable bequest gift. Similarly, the strategy of turning the tables by asking whether or not the person would feel offended if someone left them money, but had also left money to a charity was incorporated as part of the "American social norms" intervention tested previously. That intervention also appeared to have a positive effect on charitable bequest intentions. For those with substantial wealth, the Warren Buffett quote of desiring to leave his children, "Enough money so that they would feel they could do anything, but not so much that they could do nothing," might also be motivational, and might lead prospects to consider recipients other than their natural heirs.

Active modeling

- Benefit the children by charitable giving
- Pass along both value and values by modeling charitable behavior for the next generation
- Can the charity create giving opportunities where the next generation is involved?

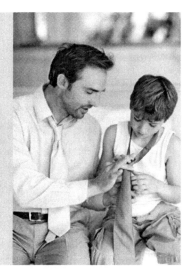

As an additional approach, some charitable giving opportunities might incorporate the heirs, not as competitors, but as participants in a continuing tradition of philanthropy. Donors may desire to benefit the children through charitable giving by passing along philanthropic values. The charity might consider how it could create opportunities to involve the next generation in the charitable process. The following example shows that this approach of involving the next generation is by no means a new idea.

Executors
become
voting
Governors
for life

4th, Each Subscriber of Twenty Pounds at one time shall be a Member for life; a Subscriber of Five Guineas per annum shall be a Governor; and a Subscriber of Fifty Pounds, or upwards, at one time, shall be a Governor for life. Governors shall be entitled to attend and vote at all the Meetings of the Committee.

5th, An Executor paying a Bequest of Fifty Pounds, shall be a Member for life; or of One Hundred Pounds, or more, a Governor for life.

The above image is taken from the public notice of the founding of the Bible Society in 1804, including a listing of the founding donors and their donation amounts. (*The Morning Post*, London, England, Monday, March 19, 1804: pg. (1); Issue 11061. 19th Century British Library Newspapers: Part II). Although the words are a bit difficult to make out, notice how the governance structure of the nonprofit organization was established. The fourth paragraph indicates "a Subscriber of Fifty Pounds, or upwards, at one time shall be a Governor for life. Governors shall be entitled to attend and vote at all the Meetings of the Committee." This shows that major donors could influence the direction of the organization. (In some sense, this is a direct exchange model of the concept applied in many nonprofit organizations today where substantial donors are commonly asked to serve as board members.) But, the fascinating part of this advertisement, for charitable bequest marketing purposes, is the 5th paragraph. It reads, "An Executor paying a Bequest of Fifty Pounds, shall be a Member for life; or of One Hundred Pounds, or more, a Governor for life."

Here we have an example of giving an organizational leadership role to the next generation by appointing the executor as a "governor for life." While, this does not mean that organizations should rework their governance structure to match this early 19th century model, there may be opportunities to involve multiple generates in administering funds donated by a decedent's estate in such a way that could be attractive to prospective bequest donors.

#2. The Ultimate Charitable Competitor

We have examined the "competition" that comes from the donor's offspring. However, there is another source of competition, which actually is a charitable competitor. It is easy to think that an organization's charitable competition is limited to other organizations supporting the same cause or in the same locality. But, in fact, the greatest charitable competitor may come from a different source.

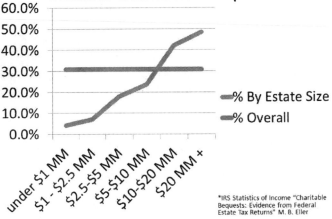

Charitable estate gifts going to the "Ultimate Charitable Competitor"

*IRS Statistics of Income "Charitable Bequests: Evidence from Federal Estate Tax Returns" M. B. Eller

The above chart shows the share of total charitable bequests dollars going to this "ultimate charitable competitor." The chart demonstrates that this competitor is particular attractive for donors with very large estates. According to the IRS statistics of income report, for estates of $20 million or more, nearly half of all charitable dollars went to this "ultimate charitable competitor."

In case it is not apparent by now, this "ultimate charitable competitor" is the private family foundation. The above statistics point out one of the reasons why an increase in total charitable bequest giving dollars may not necessarily translate directly to benefit existing nonprofits. Especially for the largest estates, a substantial share of these charitable bequest dollars will go to private family foundations.

The point here is not to be negative about the influence of such a competitor, but rather to use private family foundations as an example of a giving opportunity that takes advantage of the key psychological characteristics underlying our model of charitable bequest decision-making. Ultimately, the goal is to understand why private family foundations are so attractive and to use some of their characteristics to build our own giving opportunities for supporters of our organizations.

Dead

- Josiah K. Lilly (1948)
- Edsel Ford (1943)
- Robert Wood Johnson II (1968)
- W.K. Kellog (1951)
- Andrew W. Mellon (1937)
- John D. Rockefeller (1937)

Alive

- Lilly Endowment
- Ford Foundation
- Robert Wood Johnson Foundation
- W.K. Kellog Foundation
- Andrew W. Mellon Foundation
- The Rockefeller Foundation

Private family foundations can create great opportunities for symbolic immortality. It is common to regularly hear the names of foundations created by individuals who have long since died. These individuals, and to some extent their values, have been immortalized by the foundations they have created. In some cases, in the absence of their foundation, almost no one would have reason to recall their names. But, through their foundations, these individuals continue to influence our world and maintain a level of symbolic immortality.

Private Family Foundations: We can learn from their success

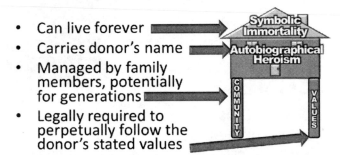

- Can live forever
- Carries donor's name
- Managed by family members, potentially for generations
- Legally required to perpetually follow the donor's stated values

Symbolic Immortality

Autobiographical Heroism

COMMUNITY

VALUES

Started during life, so creation is not subject to death-related avoidance

Consider how a private family foundation fulfills the underlying desires discussed previously. A private family foundation can live forever (thus advancing the desire for symbolic immortality). The private family foundation carries the donor's name or the donor's family's name (thus emphasizing the autobiographical heroism of the donor and the donor's family). The private family foundation is typically managed by family members and can be structured so that family members will manage the private family foundation for multiple generations to come (thus incorporating descendants into the philanthropic process). The donor can create a private family foundation to fulfill specifically selected purposes, which the foundation is legally required to perpetually follow (thus, except in very rare circumstances where the intentions are uncertain or later become contrary to public policy, the donor's values can be perpetually pursued).

Often private family foundations are created during life (although the largest transfers to the foundation may occur at death). This creation during life means that the concept of starting a private family foundation is not associated with death. Consequently, discussion of the topic is not subject to interference from the avoidance defense.

Consider developing competitive permanent giving opportunities for mid-level bequest donors

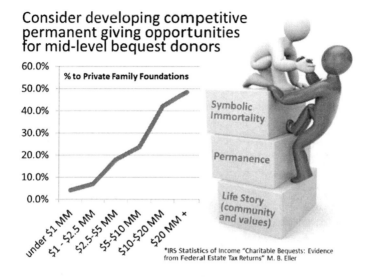

% to Private Family Foundations

Symbolic Immortality

Permanence

Life Story (community and values)

*IRS Statistics of Income "Charitable Bequests: Evidence from Federal Estate Tax Returns" M. B. Eller

Rather than bemoan the difficulty of competing with private family foundations, a more constructive approach is to consider how to develop competitive giving opportunities. These competitive opportunities, incorporating some of the characteristics of a private foundation, may be particularly attractive for mid-level bequest donors who do not see the establishment of a private family foundation as a realistic option. As reflected by the above chart, the private family foundation does not take a dominant share of the charitable bequest dollars from this mid-level market.

The private family foundation can be, not just as a challenging competitor, but a roadmap for building attractive giving opportunities. Depending upon our organizations, these opportunities may look like different types of endowed funds such as scholarships, lectureships, or permanent funds to support certain activities. Although these funds may be limited to supporting the cause of one nonprofit organization, they can incorporate many of the characteristics that make private family foundations so attractive. For example, the charity could create permanent funds bearing the name of the donor or the donor's family. Where possible, the charity might consider how family members could be involved in the administration and management of the permanent fund. A formal gift agreement may help to create a legal expectation to permanently follow the donor's stated intentions similar to the governing document of a private family foundation.

Additionally, the charity may consider encouraging the lifetime establishment of such funds in conjunction with a bequest commitment. How might this work in practice? Suppose a university had a permanent fund giving opportunity, such as a permanent named scholarship or an endowed chair with a relatively high minimum required gift. One approach to opening this opportunity to mid-level donors would be to permit the creation of the scholarship or endowed chair upon a commitment to give twice the annual payout amount each year, along with a charitable bequest commitment for the remaining amount. In this way, the endowed fund could reach its minimum level, either by virtue of accumulating the annual gifts not paid out, or by receiving a bequest gift fulfillment. In this way, the charity could legitimately have a reason to request evidence of a charitable bequest plan as a sign of a commitment to – through one means or another – reach the minimum funding level.

This is just one example of how a charity might choose to incorporate the attractive characteristics of a private family foundation into giving opportunities provided to donors. There can, of course, be a variety of additional applications depending upon the charity and the creativity and openness of the charity's leadership.

Bequest Decision-Making Process Overview

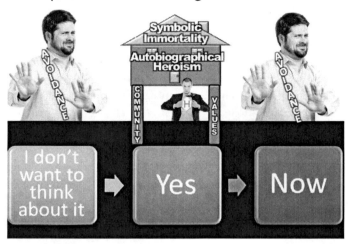

Although we have reviewed a variety of specific suggestions and strategies, the ultimate goal here is not to provide a list of pre-determined techniques. Rather, the goal has been to create a deep understanding of the charitable bequest decision-making process. From that deep understanding, we can ultimately develop new techniques and strategies precisely targeted to accomplish the goals of a specific organization working in a specific context. Now at the conclusion of this extended lecture, going inside the mind of the charitable bequest donor, I want to encourage you, dear reader, to develop the next generation of effective techniques to encourage charitable bequest planning. Take this understanding of the bequest decision-making process and use it to create dynamic approaches and strategies that we've never seen before. And, where possible, measure your results, so that you will know and you will be able to communicate the degree to which your strategies have indeed been successful. I look forward to learning about these exciting new techniques as they develop.

And finally, as I mentioned at the beginning, our

current level of understanding of the processes of charitable bequest decision-making is, I believe, gradually improving. I personally hope to continue to conduct experimental and neuroimaging research that will further our understanding of this most important decision-making process. And when another sufficiently large batch of relevant findings have accumulated, I hope to be able to communicate those to you in the future as well. Best wishes as you pursue the noble task of encouraging generosity among your fellow men and women.

REFERENCES

Bischof, M., & Bassetti, C. L. (2004). Total dream loss: A distinct neuropsychological dysfunction after bilateral PCA stroke. *Annals of Neurology, 56*, 583-586.

D'Argembeau, D., Ruby, P., Collette, F., Degueldre, C., Balteau, E., Luxen, A., & Salmon, E. (2007). Distinct regions of the medial prefrontal cortex are associated with self-referential processing and perspective taking. *Journal of Cognitive Neuroscience, 19*, 935-944.

Dechesne, M., Greenberg, J., Arndt, J., & Schimel, J. (2000). Terror managemetn and the vicissitudes of sports fan affiliation: The effects of mortality salience on optimism and fan identification. *European Journal of Social Psychology, 30*, 813-815.

Dechesne, M., Pyszczynski, T., Arndt, J., Ransom, S., Sheldon, K. M., van Knippenberg, A., et al. (2003). Literal and symbolic immortality: The effect of evidence of literal immortality on self-esteem striving in response to mortality salience. *Journal of Personality and Social Psychology, 84*, 722-737.

Denkova, E. (2006). The neural bases of autobiographical memory: How personal recollections interact with emotion and influence semantic memory (Doctoral dissertation). Retrieved from http://en.scientificcommons.org/20960088

Eller, M. B. (2001). Charitable Bequests: Evidence from Federal Estate Tax Returns. *Statistics of Income Bulletin, Spring*, Publication 1136.

Fletcher, P. C., Frith, C. D., Baker, S. C, Shallice, T., Frackowiak, R. S. J., & Dolan, R. J. (1995). The mind's eye—Precuneus activation in memory-related imagery. Neuroimage, 2, 195-200.

Freed, P. J., Yanagihara, T. K., Hirsch, J., & Mann, J. J. (2009). Neural mechanisms of grief regulation. *Biological Psychiatry, 66*(1), 33-40.

Friese, M. & Hofmann, W. (2008). What would you

have as a last supper? Thoughts about death influence evaluation and consumption of food products. *Journal of Experimental Social Psychology, 44*, 1388-1394.

Gilboa, A., Winocur, G., Grady, C. L., Hevenor, S. J., & Moscovitch, M. (2004). Remembering our past: Functional neuroanatomy of recollection of recent and very remote personal events. Cerebral Cortex, 14, 1214-1225.

Giving USA Foundation. (2012). *Giving USA 2011*. Indianapolis, IN: Author.

Greenberg, J., Kosloff, S., Solomon, S., Cohen, F., & Landau, M. J. (in press). Toward understanding the fame game: The effect of mortality salience on the appeal of fame. *Self and Identity*.

Gündel, H., O'Connor, M. F., Littrell, L., Fort, C., & Lane, R. D. (2003). Functional neuroanatomy of grief: An fMRI Study. *American Journal of Psychiatry, 160*, 1946-1953.

Harbaugh, W. T., Mayer, U., & Burghart, D. R. (2007). Neural responses to taxation and voluntary giving reveal motives for charitable donations. *Science, 316,* 1622-1625.

Hare, T. A., Camerer, C. F., Knoepfle, D. T., O'Doherty, J. P., & Rangel, A. (2010). Value computations in ventral medial prefrontal cortex during charitable decision making incorporate input from regions involved in social cognition. *Journal of Neuroscience, 30*, 583-590.

Hirschberger, G. (2010). Compassionate callousness: A terror management perspective on prosocial behavior. 201-220. In M. Mikulincer & P. R. Shaver: Eds., *Prosocial motives, emotions, and behavior: The better angels of our nature*. American Psychological Association: Washington, DC.

Hirschberger, G. (2006). Terror management and attributions of blame to innocent victims: Reconciling compassionate and defensive responses. *Journal of Personality and Social Psychology, 91*, 832-844.

Hirschberger, G., Pyszczynski, T., & Ein-Dor, T. (2009). Vulnerability and vigilance: Threat awareness and perceived adversary Intent moderate the impact of mortality salience on intergroup violence. *Personality and Social Psychology Bulletin, 35* 597-607.

Hong, Y., Wong, R. Y. M., & Liu, J. H. (2001). The history of war strengthens ethnic identification. *Journal of Psychology in Chinese Societies, 2,* 77-105.

Izuma, K., Saito, D. N., & Sadato, N. (2009). Processing of the incentive for social approval in the ventral striatum during charitable donation. *Journal of Cognitive Neuroscience, 22,* 621-631.

James, R. N., III. (2011). Charitable giving and cognitive ability. *International Journal of Nonprofit and Voluntary Sector Marketing,* 16(1), 70-83.

James, R. N., III. (2011). Cognitive skills in the charitable giving decisions of the elderly. *Educational Gerontology, 37*(7), 559-573.

James, R. N., III. (2010). Charitable estate planning and subsequent wealth accumulation: Why percentage gifts may be worth more than we thought. *International Journal of Educational Advancement, 10*(1), 24-32.

James, R. N., III. (2009). An econometric analysis of household political giving in the USA. *Applied Economics Letters, 16*(5), 539-543.

James, R.N., III (2009) Health, wealth, and charitable estate planning: A longitudinal examination of testamentary charitable giving plans. *Nonprofit and Voluntary Sector Quarterly,* 38(6), 1026-1043

James, R. N., III. (2009). The myth of the coming charitable estate windfall. *American Review of Public Administration, 39,* 661-674.

James, R. N., III. (2009). Wills, trusts, and charitable estate planning: A panel study of document effectiveness. *Financial Counseling & Planning,* 20(1), 3-14.

James, R. N., III. (2008). Charitable giving and the financial planner: Theories, findings, and implications. *Journal of Personal Finance, 6*(4), 98-117.

James, R. N., III. (2008). Distinctive characteristics of educational donors. *International Journal of Educational*

Advancement, 8(1), 3-12.

James, R. N., III, & Baker, C. (2012). Targeting wealthy donors: The dichotomous relationship of housing wealth with current and bequest giving. *International Journal of Nonprofit and Voluntary Sector Marketing, 17*(1), 25-32.

James, R. N., III, & Jones, K. S. (2011). Tithing and religious charitable giving in America. *Applied Economics*, 43(19), 2441-2450. [ISI Journal Citation Reports category: economics].

James, R. N., III., Lauderdale, M. K., & Robb, C. A. (2009). The growth of charitable estate planning among Americans nearing retirement. *Financial Services Review, 18*, 141-156.

Wiepking, P. & James, R. N., III (2013). Why are the oldest old less generous? Explanations for the unexpected age-related drop in charitable giving. *Ageing & Society, 33*(3), 486-510.

James, R. N., III., & Sharpe, D. L. (2007). The nature and causes of the U-shaped charitable giving profile. *Nonprofit and Voluntary Sector Quarterly, 36*(2), 218-238.

James, R. N., III., & Sharpe, D. L. (2007). The "sect-effect" in charitable giving: Distinctive realities of exclusively-religious charitable givers. *The American Journal of Economics and Sociology, 66*(4), 697-726.

Johnson, E. J., & Goldstein, D. (2003). Do Defaults Save Lives? Science, 302, 1338-1339.

Jonas, E., Fritsche, I., & Greenberg, J. (2005). Currencies as cultural symbols – An existential psychological perspective on reactions of Germans toward the Euro. *Journal of Economic Psychology, 26*, 129-146.

Jonas, E., Schimel, J., Greenberg, J., & Pyszczynski, T. (2002). The Scrooge Effect: Evidence that mortality salience increases prosocial attitudes and behavior. *Personality and Social Psychology Bulletin, 28*, 1342-1353.

Joireman, J. & Duell, B. (2005). Mother Teresa v. Ebenezer Scrooge: Mortality saliences leads proselfs to endorse self-transcendent values (unless proselfs are reassured). *Personality and Social Psychology Bulletin, 31*, 307-320.

Kjaer, T. W., Nowak, M., & Lou, H. C. (2002). Reflective self-awareness and conscious states: PET evidence for a common midline parietofrontal core. *Neuroimage, 17*, 1080-1086.

Kosloff, S., Greenberg, J., Weise, D., & Solomon, S. (2009). *The effects of mortality salience on political preferences: The roles of charisma and political orientation.* Manuscript in preparation

Landau, M. J., Greenberg, J., & Sullivan, D. (2009). *Defending a coherent autobiography: When past events appear incoherent, mortality salience prompts compensatory bolstering of the past's significance and the future's orderliness.* Manuscript in preparation.

Landau, M. J., Greenberg, J., & Sullivan, D. (2009). Managing terror when self-worth and wordviews collide: Evidence that mortality salience increases reluctance to self-enhance beyond authorities. *Journal of Experimental Social Psychology, 45*, 68-79.

Lieberman, J. D., Arndt, J., Personius, J., & Cook, A. (2001). Vicarious annihilation: The effect of mortality salience on perceptions of hate crimes. *Law and Human Behavior, 25*, 547-566.

Lou, H. C., Luber, B., Crupain, M., Keenan, J. P., Nowak, M., & Kjaer, T. W. (2004). Parietal cortex and representation of the mental self. *Proceedings of the National Academy of Sciences, 101*, 6827-6832.

Maddock, R. J., Garrett, A. S., Buonocore, M. H. (2003). Posterior cingulate cortex activation by emotional words: fMRI evidence from a valence decision task. *Human Brain Mapping, 18*, 30-41.

Meulenbroek, O., Rijpkema, M., Kessels, R., Rikkert, M., & Fernández, G. (2010). Autobiographical memory retrieval in patients with Alzheimer's disease. NeuroImage, 53, 331-340.

Moll, J., Kreuger, F., Zahn, R., Pardini, M., Oliveira-

Souza, R., & Grafman, J. (2006). Human front-mesolimbic networks guide decisions about charitable donation. *Proceedings of the National Academy of Sciences, 103*, 15623-15629.

National Committee on Planned Giving (2001) *Planned Giving in the United States, 2000: A Survey of Donors*. Author: Indianapolis, Indiana.

Nederhof, A. 1985. Methods of coping with social desirability bias: a review. European Journal of Social Psychology, 15(3):263-280.

Norenzayan, A., & Hansen, I. G. (2006). Belief in supernatural agents in the face of death. *Personality and Social Psychology Bulletin, 32*, 174-187.

Pharoah, C. (2010). Charity Market Monitor 2010: Tracking the funding of UK charities. London: CaritasData

Rabin, J. S., Gilboa, A., Stuss, D. T., Mar, R. A., & Rosenbaum, R. S. (2010). Common and unique neural correlates of autobiographical memory and theory of mind. *Journal of Cognitive Neuroscience, 22*, 1095-1111.

Renkema, L. J., Stapel, D. A., Maringer, M., Van Yperen, N. W. (2008). Terror management and stereotyping: Why do people stereotype when mortality is salient? *Personality and Social Psychology Bulletin, 34*, 553-564.

Pyszczynski, T., Abdollahi, A., Solomon, S., Greenberg, J., Cohen, F., & Weise, D. (2006). Mortality salience, martyrdom, and military might: The Great Satan versus the Axis of Evil. *Personality and Social Psychology Bulletin, 32*, 525-537.

Pyszcznski, T., Greenberg, J., & Solomon, S. (1999). A dual process model of defense against conscious and unconscious death-related thoughts: An extension of terror management theory. *Psychological Review, 106*, 835-845.

Rosen, M. (2010). *Donor-Centered Planned Gift Marketing*. Wiley & Sons.

Routledge, C. & Arndt, J. (2008). Self-sacrifice as self-defense: Mortality salience increases efforts to affirm a symbolic immortal self at the expense of the physical self. *European Journal of Social Psychology, 38*, 531-541.

Routley, C. J. (2011). Leaving a charitable legacy: Social influence, the self and symbolic immortality (Unpublished doctoral dissertation). University of the West of England, Bristol, UK.

Schimel, J., Simon, L., Greenberg, J., Pyszczynski, T., Solomon, S., Waxmonski, J., et al. (1999). Stereotypes and terror management: Evidence that mortality salience enhances stereotypic thinking and preferences. *Journal of Personality and Social Psychology, 77*, 905-926.

Viard, A., Piolino, P., Desgranges, B., Chételat, G., Lebreton, K., Landeau, B., & Eustache, F. (2007). Hippocampal activation for autobiographical memories over the entire lifetime in healthy aged subjects: An fMRI study. Cerebral Cortex, 17, 2453-2467.

Vogeley, K., & Fink, G. R. (2003). Neural correlates of the first-person-perspective [Review]. *Trends in Cognitive Science, 7*, 38-42.

Vovelle, M. (1980). A century and one-half of American epitaphs (1660-1813): Toward the study of collective attitudes about death. *Comparative Studies in Society and History, 22*(4), 534-547.

Wade-Benzoni, K. A., Tost, L. P., Hernandez, M., & Larrick, R. P. (2012). It's only a matter of time: Death, legacies and intergenerational decisions. *Psychological Science, 23*(7), 704-709.

Zagorsky, J. L. (2012). Do people save or spend their inheritances? Understanding what happens to inherited wealth. *Journal of Family and Economic Issues, DOI 10.1007/s10834-012-9299-y*

ABOUT THE AUTHOR

Russell James, J.D., Ph.D., CFP® is a professor in the Department of Personal Financial Planning at Texas Tech University where he serves as the Director of Graduate Studies in Charitable Planning and is the CH Foundation Chair in Personal Financial Planning. He teaches graduate level Charitable Gift Planning courses both in the Department of Personal Financial Planning and at the Texas Tech University School of Law, and previously taught a graduate course in Functional Magnetic Resonance Imaging (fMRI) Study Design and Analysis. He holds a J.D., *cum laude*, from the University of Missouri School of Law where he received the United Missouri Bank Award for Most Outstanding Work in Gift and Estate Taxation and Planning. His Ph.D. in Consumer and Family Economics is from the University of Missouri, where his dissertation was on the topic of charitable giving.

Dr. James received the 2012 Outstanding Teacher of the Year award from the Texas Tech Personal Financial Planning Student Association, and previously received the Outstanding Teacher of the Year award at the University of Georgia. In addition to his work as a professor, Dr. James has worked as an estate planning attorney, as a director of planned giving, and as a college president.

His research focuses on uncovering practical methods to encourage generosity and satisfaction in financial decision-making. Dr. James has over 145 publications in academic journals, conference proceedings, books, and professional periodicals. He has presented his research as an invited speaker at universities in the U.S., England, Scotland, Ireland, Germany, Spain, and The Netherlands and at organizations including the American Cancer Society, World Wildlife Fund, Community Foundation of Ireland, and Giving Korea. He has been quoted on financial and charitable topics in a variety of media outlets including *The New York Times, The Wall Street Journal, CNN, MSNBC, CNBC, Bloomberg News, ABC News, U.S. News & World Report,* and *USA Today.*

His research has been published in a wide variety of academic research journals including Ageing & Society, American Journal of Economics and Sociology, The American Review of Public Administration, Applied Economics, Applied Economics Letters, Educational Gerontology, Nonprofit and Voluntary Sector Quarterly, International Journal of Nonprofit and Voluntary Sector Marketing, International Journal of Educational Advancement, Financial Counseling & Planning, Financial Services Review, Journal of Personal Finance, International Journal of Consumer Studies, Environment & Behavior, Social Indicators Research, the Journal of Consumer Affairs, and several others.

CPSIA information can be obtained at www.ICGtesting.com
Printed in the USA
LVOW101144050613

337074LV00001B/25/P